Scotstyle

100 YEARS OF SCOTTISH ARCHITECTURE
(1916-2015)

Edited by Neil Baxter and Fiona Sinclair

First published 2016 by
The Royal Incorporation of Architects in Scotland

Text: Neil Baxter Hon FRIAS, Iain Dickson PPRIAS, Helen Kendrick, Euan Leitch, Ranald MacInnes, Ruairidh Moir RIAS,
Sarah Pearce, Fiona Sinclair FRIAS, Frank Walker OBE FRIAS and Andrew P K Wright OBE PPRIAS.
Design: Jon Jardine (mail@jonjardine.com)

ISBN 978-1-873190-71-5

Printed in the UK by Bell & Bain Ltd, Glasgow

A catalogue record for this book is available from the British Library

We are very grateful to the following people and organisations for the use of the photographs in this book: Canmore, Scran, the Scottish Instagram
community (particularly Grant Bulloch FRIAS), Scotland's leading architectural photographers (individual credits accompany each image).

Every effort has been made to obtain copyright clearance on all the images within this publication.
Please address any enquiries to Neil.Baxter@rias.org.uk

Contents

Note

Because of issues around the accurate dating of projects, the description by Frank Walker OBE FRIAS of the Nuffield Transplantation Surgery Unit has been moved into the decade 1967-1975. To maintain our "ten buildings per decade" chapter form the description by Andrew PK Wright OBE PPRIAS of St Peter's College now sits at the end of the preceding section.

Preface

THIS BOOK AND THE EXHIBITION of the same name which it was written to accompany, marks the centenary of one event and is inspired by another.

In 1916, a group of elderly Scots architects convened in Edinburgh to make ambitious plans. While the First World War continued to rage in France, their discussions were conceived in the optimistic expectation of a better future. What emerged, with a view to building for the decades to come, was a new organisation for the promotion of Scottish architecture. On the second of November 1916 what would, in time, become The Royal Incorporation of Architects in Scotland (RIAS) was born.

Decades later, in the early 1980s, inspired by an original idea from the architect Kit Campbell, the, by now very well established, Royal Incorporation decided to mark the 150th birthday in 1984 of its sister institute, The Royal Institute of British Architects (RIBA). A major touring exhibition and a book, celebrating the best buildings in Scotland from each of the previous 150 years, were planned.

With characteristic gusto, the RIAS Secretary, Charles McKean, convened a distinguished panel of architects and historians. He also persuaded the, very young, Glasgow architect, Fiona Sinclair, to script the exhibition and to write the

accompanying book. Over 750 public nominations were whittled down to the final selection by the jury, expertly steered by then RIAS President, John Richards.

The exhibition was the most substantial and significant celebration of the RIBA's anniversary in 1984. In fact, it and the book *Scotstyle: 150 Years of Scottish Architecture* were as substantial as anything the Institute itself did to mark its major milestone.

The celebration of the RIAS' centenary seemed an ideal moment to revisit *Scotstyle*, to review the previous choices and bring the list up to date. For 2016 it was agreed, on the wise advice of the

Scottish Government's Chief Architect, Ian Gilzean, that, rather than trying to find one building for each year, ten buildings per decade would offer a better opportunity to truly recognise the best from a century of architectural evolution.

As with the first exhibition only buildings which are still standing were considered (in 1984 an exception was made for the Glasgow Empire Exhibition of 1938, on the pretext that its buildings were always intended to be temporary). Once again public nominations were received (over 400) and an expert panel of ten historians and architects was brought together. This time they also became the authors, under the superb convenorship of the most suitable candidate for the task, the highly talented Fiona Sinclair.

Scotstyle 2016 is a significantly different list from the 1984 version. Some highlights recur, some choices are simply different and sadly some gems have been demolished in the interim. There are, of course, three new decades of brilliant Scottish architectural treasures to be found here.

The last century has witnessed the most significant and substantial technological change of any period in human history. This volume amply demonstrates that Scottish architects have risen to its opportunities. A combination of design talent, innovation and sheer quality continues to characterise the best of our architecture and to improve the lives of all of Scotland's people. What differs from previous eras is the context of support of Scotland's architects from our very own membership organisation, the RIAS. So welcome to *Scotstyle 2016*, happy birthday to the Royal Incorporation and here's to the next 100 glorious years!

David Dunbar PPRIAS
Chair, Festival of Architecture 2016

Introduction

In 1984, in the introduction to *Scotstyle: 150 Years of Scottish Architecture*, Colin McWilliam set out a narrative that sensibly (and rather remarkably) connected the 145 buildings featured. Observing that the selection process had followed the rather arbitrary pattern of one building per year, he wisely steered clear of drawing conclusions (in particular, over whether the entries were definitively Scottish in style). Instead he made a series of interesting statistical observations, analysing the buildings in terms of geographic location and type.

What McWilliam did not reveal was that not only was the pattern arbitrary, but that it was, to a significant degree, manipulated. So rich in architectural pickings were certain periods (for instance, the mid 1850s in Glasgow) that buildings too good to be dropped from the selection were shuffled from date of design, to commencement and, failing that, completion. Taking more than forty years to build, the extraordinary St

Conan's Kirk on Loch Awe was slotted into a handy gap (as it happened, 1927). Charles Rennie Mackintosh's Glasgow School of Art had only just begun on the date under which it appeared (1897), ensuring that John A Campbell's Northern Assurance Building on Glasgow's St Vincent Street could find a home under the Art School's date of completion (1909).

The result of this delicate balancing act of 150 years of Scottish design and construction was the "architectural cake rather than ... bread and butter" to which McWilliam's preface referred. With the understandable exception of the lean years of the Second World War (where a five-year span was represented by a single – yet heroic – building, the Italian Chapel on Lamb Holm), the selected entries earned their places in the face of fierce competition. Despite their appearance on this 1984 roll of honour, however, eleven of the buildings have subsequently been either completely or partially demolished,

and a further five are seriously at risk.

Assessing a group of buildings selected as representative of a decade rather than a single year better illustrates typology and stylistic developments. The original *Scotstyle* made curious bedfellows out of farm steadings and glasshouses; churches and railway stations; lighthouses and mausolea. The Arts and Crafts-inspired, stone-built, slate-roofed East Suffolk Road Halls of Residence (1916) lay sandwiched between two utilitarian examples of early in-situ concrete construction (Weir's Administration Building in Cathcart, and the long-gone Crosslee Cordite Factory near Houston). This time around, it more happily rubs shoulders with the romantic Cour House in Argyll and the idiosyncratic Dutch Village in the Fife countryside. And against all the odds, the decade encompassing the Second World War is now the most assuredly and consistently stylistic of all.

In 1984, the selection was book-ended (quite literally) by two great public institutions, William Playfair's extension to the Royal Scottish Academy in Edinburgh (1834), and the Burrell Collection in Glasgow's Pollok Park (1983). Built for the display of fine art and artefacts, both are publicly accessible yet nonetheless manage to reinforce the notion that 'architecture' is experienced at arm's length. Now, in this year of centenary celebrations, the bookends are instead two housing projects of clear architectural and social ambition: urban exemplars offering an inclusive and exciting future.

McWilliam found the 1984 survey of what he dubbed a "no-man's land of taste" evenly distributed across the country. He remarked that, "outside the big towns Strathclyde (21) and Tayside (12) are well ahead, leaving the other regions in single figures and Dumfries and Galloway nowhere." Happily, (and less through local authority re-organisation than through the emergence of strong local talent), this most southerly of regions is now better represented. However the real success story is the emergence of significant new buildings on the islands, Tiree, Skye, Orkney and Bute.

Of the original 145 buildings illustrated in *Scotstyle*, 56 were eligible for reinclusion, although in the event, only 37 have made a re-appearance. The pre-war decades have seen little change – few architects can match the end-of-career conviction exhibited by Lorimer, Burnet and Miller (and few the creative energy of a young Jack Coia or Basil Spence) – but from the late 1930s and early 40s emerge two hidden gems in Aberdeen, and the succeeding decade revealed the inexplicable omission first time around of the National Library of Scotland.

Selections from the 1960s and 70s now better represent the popularity concrete enjoyed in the hands of the nation's architects (and engineers), with its use decorative and structural, parabolic and plain, in-situ and precast. But the final decade celebrated in the original *Scotstyle* contained a number of buildings so perfectly of their time that they could not fail but be included once more. They mostly share an innovative quality that has undoubtedly influenced the architects that followed.

In large part down to its relatively recent urban renaissance (not to mention the effect of the 1999 City of Architecture celebrations and the 2014 Commonwealth Games), Glasgow now chalks up an impressive 36 entries (only one less than in 1984), whereas Edinburgh is represented by a significantly reduced 19 projects. What it lacks in numbers, however, the capital more than makes up for in being represented by two big-hitters, the National Museum of Scotland (1998) and the Scottish Parliament (2004). Along with Sir Robert Lorimer's gutsy Scottish National War Memorial (1927) and Thomas Tait's superb St Andrew's House (1939), these four national institutions alone could tell a coherent stylistic tale of the last 100 years, whereas in the west, the breakout buildings are less easily classified.

With the years between 1834 and 1915 now excluded from the dialogue, there are fewer banking halls, country houses and monuments built for the hell of it, and no farm buildings, sluice houses or railway stations in the mix. Furthermore, there are fewer schools (only two, in fact), but an increased number of buildings created in celebration of the visual arts, performance and quiet contemplation. Tourism, and the promotion of the nation's attractions and collections through purpose-built facilities in both countryside and city, emerges as an important initiative. And while the 1875 Kibble Palace glasshouse in Glasgow has fallen off the list, the equally elegant John Hope Gateway (2009) in Edinburgh's Royal Botanic Gardens has nicely filled its place, with the popular Princes Square on Buchanan Street (1987) similarly occupying the spot vacated by Jenners' Store on Princes Street (1895).

Arguably, the glorious eccentricity of Templeton's Carpet Factory on Glasgow Green (1889) or Dundee's Cox's Stack (1865) is missed, but instead there is a one-man castle built of in-situ concrete, sand and shell on Loch Inver (1950), and a former horse-drawn tram depot converted for exploratory drama at Tramway (2000). There are fewer churches (now, just six, the most recent opened in 2012), and instead there are cathedrals to the newspaper industry (1936), hydroelectric power (1934), and tobacco (1949).

There are now houses (and a church, and parliament) on whose roofs turf and sedum have been planted. With the early 1990s, allied to this growth in organic architecture, came a resurgence in the use of public sculpture. The use of contemporary sculpture in the remarkable urban block, the Italian Centre in Glasgow (1991), has yet to be bettered in the city.

But of all the building types represented – housing, industry, commerce, education, research, arts, leisure and worship – it is healthcare that has consistently encouraged architects to raise their game. The first UK hospital built after the Second World War at Vale of Leven (1951) may no longer appear cutting-edge, but the country's Maggie's Centres are consistently exceptional, with two of the most sublime represented.

Of course, an analysis of 100 years of Scottish architecture throws up changes in politics, patronage and production. Despite a strong showing from Aberdeen and Argyll, this selection features less indigenous granite and sandstone than it does homegrown timber, imported brick and copper. Slate now hangs from walls as well as sitting on roofs, and there is an emphasis on recycled (and recyclable) materials, sustainability and sophisticated services.

Consistent, however, across the last century's buildings (or, at least, those featured here), is an abiding (some might say) inexplicable attraction to the flat (or very shallow) roof. Of the 100 buildings featured, over half have flat roofs, as if in denial of the nation's changeable weather. However most of these buildings are still fairly intact and serving their original, or a new, function well. So, flat roofed or pitched, Scotland's architects – and builders – continue to design for posterity.

Of course the Scotland that our architects continue to shape is much changed over the last century. Public patronage has been fizzed up with lottery funding, enlivening our arts and cultural built landscape. However, no change has been more significant that the devolved, confident, governance following the

Scotland Act of 1998. The Parliament building, though more 'marmite' than any other of recent times, is deservedly here.

The Scottish Parliament was recognised in one of the first RIAS Andrew Doolan Best Building in Scotland Awards. The RIAS has also, more recently, launched its own national awards for Scotland. As well as bestowing laurels on an annual 'top ten' (or thereabouts) the RIAS Awards also recognise the increasingly ingenious use of timber, energy efficiency, sustainability and conservation best practice, as well

as emerging architects and perhaps, most significantly, the crucial role of the client in any successful work of architecture. There are 100 buildings in this book – that's a whole lot of inspired clients encouraging and supporting their architects to excel.

Neil Baxter Hon FRIAS
and Fiona Sinclair FRIAS
April 2016

Iain Dickson PPRIAS

IAIN DICKSON GRADUATED from the Scott Sutherland School of Architecture in 1976 having studied History of Architecture as his major subject. He was then successively assistant, architect, partner and senior partner of George Watt and Stewart in Aberdeen. Although a small practice it is now the oldest firm of architects in Aberdeen still practising in its original guise, having been established in 1909.

Iain has always had a keen interest in his professional body, The Royal Incorporation of Architects in Scotland (RIAS) having served in various capacities at both committee and RIAS Council level. He was President of the Royal Incorporation from 1999 to 2001. Since retiring from practice at the end of 2010 he has worked as a part time academic at the Scott Sutherland School of Architecture, Aberdeen.

1916-1925

ESSAYS BY IAIN DICKSON PPRIAS

Rosyth Garden City

Queensferry Road, Fife

Greig & Fairbairn and AH Mottram

PRIOR TO THE FIRST WORLD WAR, the Royal Navy did not have a substantial east coast base to counter the threat of the German Fleet. The construction of the Rosyth Naval Dockyard began in 1909 with over a thousand men employed there. Accommodation for these workers was in corrugated iron huts in an area known as Tin Town. The huts were demolished in the 1920s.

Clearly, permanent accommodation was required for dockyard workers. The Scottish National Housing Company (the forerunner of the Scottish Special Housing Association) was formed to build the Rosyth Garden Village along similar lines to the principles established by Ebenezer Howard in the 1902 republication of his *Garden Cities of Tomorrow*.

Raymond Unwin had been one of the chief architects of both the Hampstead and Letchworth Garden Cities, and it was one of his pupils, AH Mottram, who was appointed to oversee the work at Rosyth. Work began in 1915, and the first house was occupied by May 1916. While Greig and Fairburn of Edinburgh designed the first 150 houses, Mottram was responsible for many of the remainder. In total, 1,700 houses were built.

A pleasant garden suburb was created with rings of tree-lined crescents and avenues surrounding a central park. Houses with front and back gardens were grouped in clusters of two up to six houses with dormers and projecting gables. To reduce the scale of development further, differing materials were used to provide variety – brick, render, slate and tile. Churches, schools and shops were added over the years.

The 'New Town' of Rosyth may not seem exceptional today, but it heralded the way forward for much of Scotland's public housing in the twentieth century.

Rosyth Garden City

Suffolk Road Halls of Residence

East Suffolk Road, Newington, Edinburgh

Alan K Robertson

IN THE EARLY TWENTIETH century there was very little accommodation for female students enrolled at Edinburgh University or one of its colleges. The provision of purpose-built accommodation for female students was mooted as early as 1906, but it took a decade until the first phase at East Suffolk Road was completed. They were the first student halls of residence in Scotland built exclusively for women.

Alan K Robertson of Robertson and Swan was appointed to design the buildings. Earlier, he had designed the Edinburgh Provincial Training Centre (now Paterson's Land) for the same client. The original intention was to have seven hostels, but only three were completed in the first phase – Buchanan, Playfair and Balfour Halls.

The buildings are reminiscent of Robert Lorimer (for whom Swan had worked) having an Arts and Crafts air, all satisfyingly grouped around a large lawn. The buildings have dominant mansard roofs with plain and decorative dormers.

Incorporating Craigleith stone, the elevations comprise advanced gabled porches, bow windows and have many small-paned windows. Brick and harling are used on the rear elevations.

After the war, Robertson and Swan did not continue in practice. Robertson took Frank Wood into partnership and he completed the final two Halls – Darroch and Carlyle. Robertson died from his war wounds in 1925 and did not see the scheme completed. The two final Halls were opened in 1928.

The following year it was stated of the project:

"It is unique in character and unique in setting. No similar scheme existing in Scotland, and few groups of womens students' residencies in England can show such well arranged buildings or more ample recreation grounds".

Suffolk Road Halls of Residence

Dutch Village, Craigtoun Park

St Andrews, Fife

Paul Waterhouse

CLOSE TO ST ANDREWS sits the former Mount Melville Estate, owned from the late seventeenth to the early twentieth century by the family of General George Melville of Strathkinness. In 1901, the estate was purchased by the brewing magnate Dr James Younger of Alloa. It was sold to Fife County Council in 1947 and its name changed to Craigtoun. It later became Scotland's first public country park.

A great deal of architectural work was carried out during the early twentieth century – gardens, avenues, lakes and the fairytale Dutch Village built on a small island in one of the ornamental lakes. Approached via a pedestrian bridge of three arches, there is a two-storey gatehouse, a boathouse and a summerhouse.

Viewed from a distance it is reminiscent of the chateaux in the Loire Valley where the buildings are reflected in the water. However, there the similarity ends as the buildings in the Dutch Village are white harled with red pantiled roofs. The buildings are enclosed and linked together by perimeter walls and a columned loggia. Close by is a grotto and a series of three cascades.

The architect, Paul Waterhouse, was from a dynastic architectural family. His father had been President of the RIBA, as was he and also his son. In addition, he was related by marriage to the Younger family, hence the commission. He died four years after the Dutch Village was completed.

Over the years, the Dutch Village has fallen into disrepair. However, the lake was drained in late 2015 with a view to carrying out surveys of the foundations and to establish a programme of restoration.

Cour House

Mull of Kintyre, Argyll

Oliver Hill

ARCHITECT, AUTHOR AND LONDONER, Hill had many Scottish connections. His family originally came from Aberdeenshire and he was apprenticed to the Scottish architect William Flockhart for three years. More pertinently, Hill was also a friend and admirer of Sir Edwin Lutyens, whose influence is evident at Cour House.

One of his first major country house commissions, Hill chose an English mediaeval style for Cour. However, it is not as simple as that, as there are overtones of the Arts and Crafts movement about this house as well. Not only that, it incorporates some modern features – providing a foretaste of Hill's

International Modernism of a decade later.

The greatest achievement at Cour is how the building nestles into its site and appears to rise out of the ground. The roughly symmetrical entrance front is relatively low and belies the fact that at the rear the landscape steps down

Cour House
© Crown Copyright: Historic Environment Scotland. Licensor canmore.org.uk

towards the sea. The plan is essentially 'L'-shaped with re-entrant, beehive-roofed towers holding the wings in place. The whole composition is crowned by a series of massive roofs bringing all the components together.

Generally two-storey, there are single-storey service wings; the massing is varied in that there are both horizontal and vertical elements in the elevational treatment; soaring, massive, battered masonry chimney stacks visually break the roofline and add interest. Daylight is provided through horizontal bands of mullioned windows. The grey-green whinstone was quarried on the site; the slates are from Purbeck; the windows are metal casements.

Stylistically, Cour is a conundrum – it looks both to history and the future. However, it is relaxed and romantic in a wonderful setting and is perhaps best described as *individual*.

Zoology Building, University of Glasgow
© Jean O'Reilly

Zoology Building, University of Glasgow

University Avenue, Glasgow

Sir John James Burnet with Norman A Dick

SIR JOHN GRAHAM KERR, Regius Professor of Zoology at Glasgow University from 1902 to 1935, was instrumental in the development of a dedicated Zoology Building for the university. The facility was originally located in the basement of the Hunterian Museum, so the new building had to be close to it and with dedicated lecture theatre, laboratories and museum.

The development was confirmed in 1914, but with the outbreak of war contracts were not exchanged until 1921. By this stage, Burnet was working from his London practice much of the time, so, while he designed the overall proposal,

his Glasgow partner Norman Aitken Dick carried out much of the work. John Watson Junior (son of John Watson, architect of Glasgow's City Chambers extension) also assisted on the project.

The scale of the building belies its size as the various elements are broken up and cannot be readily viewed together. The entrance elevation is small but monumental: it has Baroque details with much use of channelled ashlar; a broken pediment surmounts the doorway. To the left of the entrance is a blank wall forming the rear of the lecture theatre with a tall, decorative louvred cupola ventilator

above; to the right, at first floor level, is a range of three windows separated by squat dwarf pilasters.

The elevation to the laboratory wing comprises a modern façade with wide bays separated by masonry mullions with windows stretching up through two storeys and incorporating chequered spandrel panels at the intermediate floor. The return elevation to the lecture theatre has three windows whose stepping cills accompany the steep rake of the lecture theatre. This is Burnet at his best (with a little help from his friends).

Arches and Extension, City Chambers

John Street, Glasgow

Watson, Salmond and Gray

THE EASTERN EXTENSION TO Glasgow's City Chambers was the subject of an open competition which was won by Watson and Salmond in 1913. Subsequently, Gray was taken into partnership although the work is attributed to John Watson. Delayed by the First World War, the extension was not completed until 1923.

The design comprised a block of four storeys with basement and attic whose principal elevation to Cochrane Street is of ten bays in a rigid Greek manner. The six central bays are grouped within a colonnade of soaring Ionic columns over the first and second floors. The bays to either side project from the plane of the façade to emphasise the location of the entrance doorways; the end bays return along the side elevations. A heavy cornice pulls the composition together and supports the floor above which is set back to give an attic effect; there is much effective use of channelled ashlar. The massing of the elements is essentially symmetrical, although the detail varies in corresponding bays.

The extension is linked to William Young's City Chambers by a pair of supremely elegant French Renaissance-inspired arches in the style of François Mansart. Tall central arches are flanked by smaller pedestrian arches on either side, separated from one another by pairs of fluted Ionic columns sitting on a polished ashlar base. Detached urns sit above the columns, backed by a deep parapet behind which is a high level, top-lit corridor. The main arches are surmounted by elaborate cartouches. They create an elegant connection between the original building and its successor.

In 1927, Watson, Salmond and Gray won the first RIBA Scottish Architecture Medal for the best city building completed since 1922 for this project.

Arches and Extension, City Chambers

TOP AND RIGHT

© Jon Jardine

ABOVE MIDDLE, ABOVE BOTTOM

© Jean O'Reilly

McLaren Warehouse
RIGHT
© Jon Jardine
OPPOSITE PAGE
© Jean O'Reilly

McLaren Warehouse

George Square, Glasgow

James Miller

PERTHSHIRE-BORN JAMES MILLER was one of the most prolific and successful Scottish architects of all time. He had been strongly influenced by North American architecture since the turn of the century but never travelled there; he learnt from associates and contemporary journals. From the early 1900s, his work echoed the emerging steel-framed buildings of Chicago and Montreal.

By the end of the First World War, Miller was approaching sixty, but producing a confident urban neo-baroque style, exemplified by the McLaren Warehouse on the south side of George Square. With overtones of the Canadian Northern Station in Montreal, it is stylistically similar to his own Union Bank building on St Vincent Street.

Seven storeys with basement, the steel frame is clad in pale sandstone, the design regrettably unfinished on the principal frontage to George Square. There are seven bays along Hanover Street, and only five to George Square, half the intended length. The ground and first floors form a base, separated from the remaining upper storeys by a masonry entablature and band course.

Huge doorways are provided at the centre of the Hanover Street elevation and on the extreme right bay of the George Square façade (where originally intended to be central). Above, the metal-framed glazed bays extend through the upper five storeys with bronze spandrels at each floor. The façades are capped with a deep cornice supported on pairs of huge console brackets, while the two main corners are emphasised by a greater use of masonry punctured with windows expressed individually.

Had it been completed, this would have been an inter-war classic. In its truncated form, it is still deserving of its location on the city's principal public square.

1924

Bandstand and Amphitheatre

Kelvingrove Park, Glasgow

Glasgow Corporation Parks Department

KELVINGROVE, THE FIRST PLANNED public park in Scotland, staged three international exhibitions in 1888, 1901 and 1911, attracting more than 25 million visitors in total. Each of those exhibitions had temporary bandstands of the traditional octagonal shape.

The current bandstand, opened in 1924, is one of only three in Scotland with an amphitheatre, and the only original bandstand left in Glasgow. At the height of its popularity there was seating for 3,000 and standing room for 7,000. It occupied a picturesque location immediately adjacent to the River Kelvin, the oval amphitheatre making use of the natural slope of the land rising up from the river.

The bandstand has a symmetrical theatre layout comprising a projecting stage with a small service area and centrally located gabled projection behind. The stage has a central door to the rear with flanking doors in angled corners on either side. Brick-built with whitewashed render and half-timbering, the building has a red brick base and window dressings, and corniced string course.

The piended roof has overhanging bracketed eaves, red tile brattishing, and a centrally located ridge vent with cupola and capped with a decorative finial. The stage is framed by tapered Ionic columns, and a canopy is provided over the performance area, supported on scroll brackets. At the top of the amphitheatre are two pay kiosks built later on an axis with the bandstand.

A 1992 proposal to demolish the bandstand met with huge public opposition, despite which it closed in 1999. Subsequently, the bandstand, amphitheatre and kiosks have been conserved and sensitively repaired – the bandstand provided with enhanced facilities. It re-opened in May 2014, in nice time for Glasgow's hugely successful Commonwealth Games.

Winter Gardens Pavilion

Victoria Street, Rothesay, Isle of Bute
Alexander Stephen and Walter MacFarlane & Co

ROTHESAY AS A HOLIDAY destination and the Winter Gardens as its seafront centrepiece declined from the 1960s. The town is ancient – Rothesay Castle dates back to the thirteenth century, and is also unique as the only circular castle in Scotland.

In its heyday, the Winter Gardens had a capacity of 1,100 but by 1983 its use had diminished and the Town Council sought to demolish it. After a public enquiry the Secretary of State disallowed the demolition as the building had been listed of historic interest since 1978. In the 1990s it was redeveloped as a tourist information centre and cinema.

In late Victorian times an octagonal bandstand stood on the esplanade gardens. When the development of the Winter Gardens commenced, it was incorporated into the new building as its stage. With a nod to the nearby castle, a circular plan form was adopted for the pavilion.

A 25-metre diameter glass dome half envelops the bandstand; opposite is the entrance, formed by a curved portico flanked by two square pagoda-roofed towers. The dome is supported on radial steel ribs culminating in a central boss. Excellent detail abounds – cast iron handrails and lamp standards, art nouveau panelling, cartouches and finials, internal and external promenades. It is an exciting example of seaside architectural flamboyance.

Alex Stephen was the Rothesay Burgh Surveyor; Walter MacFarlane & Company's Saracen Foundry designed and fabricated the steelwork, which was shipped across the Clyde. The pavilion is an important survivor of this prominent Glasgow firm's work. In 2015, concern was expressed that the building's fabric was once again deteriorating. An enduring solution must be found to allow the Winter Gardens to survive and be enjoyed by future generations.

Winter Gardens Pavilion
© Crown Copyright: Historic Environment Scotland.
Licensor canmore.org.uk

War Memorial and Cowdray Hall

Schoolhill, Aberdeen

A Marshall Mackenzie and AGR Mackenzie

THIS EXTENSION TO Matthews & Mackenzie's Art Gallery and Gray's School of Art of 1885 (with Sculpture Court of 1905) occupies the corner of Aberdeen's Schoolhill and Blackfriars Street. Originally, it was intended to build a memorial to Edward VII alongside a public hall. Planning began but was delayed by war; thereafter it became the city's War Memorial, funded by public subscription, and with the adjoining public hall paid for by Lord Cowdray. A Marshall Mackenzie carried out the initial work; after the war he was assisted by his son, AGR Mackenzie, himself wounded in service.

A particularly fine example of neo-classical work of the period, the war memorial comprises a restrained concave quadrant. Creating the curve is a colonnade of six tall Corinthian columns silhouetted against an inscribed wall under a heavy entablature – all in severe grey granite to underline the solemn purpose of the memorial.

War Memorial and Cowdray Hall
© Crown Copyright: Historic Environment Scotland.
Licensor canmore.org.uk

To either side of the quadrant are angled bays, each containing entrance doors – one to the Cowdray Hall, the other to the memorial court. Above both swagged doorways are lofty blind panels. Sitting within the quadrant, flanked by steps, is a massive dignified lion sculpture by William McMillan.

Inside, and largely unseen by the public, is a beautiful, octagonal, marble-clad hall of remembrance with balustraded balcony, filled with light from the cupola atop the dome. Steel-framed and clad in copper, this is the feature that gives emphasis to the memorial and articulates the street corner.

In contrast to the starkness of the principal façade, the Blackfriars Street elevation to the public hall has a blind portico and pilasters over a rusticated base, the trimmings in pink granite against a grey background.

Fiona Sinclair FRIAS

FIONA SINCLAIR IS A Fellow of the Royal
Incorporation of Architects in Scotland,
a conservation-accredited architect and
sometime author and historian. She has
twice been elected President of the
Glasgow Institute of Architects, and
was a member of the Historic Buildings
Council for Scotland. She is author
of *Scotstyle – 150 Years of Scottish
Architecture*, co-author of the *RIAS
Architectural Guide to North Clyde
Estuary*, and the Penguin *Buildings of
Scotland* volumes *Argyll and Bute* and
Lanarkshire and Renfrewshire.

Fiona serves on the Kilallan Kirk
Preservation Trust, and as Director of
the Formakin Estate Garden Company.
She has worked on the care and repair
of a range of historic buildings, including
scheduled ancient monuments, churches,
country houses, estate cottages,
designed landscapes, tenements, a
synagogue, a medieval town house and a
malt whisky distillery.

1926-1935

ESSAYS BY FIONA SINCLAIR FRIAS

1927

Scottish National War Memorial

Edinburgh Castle, Edinburgh

Sir Robert Lorimer

PAINFUL IN SUBJECT – a tribute to the many Scots who fell during the First World War – and painful, too, for the architect, who cannot have imagined the controversy and public debate that would accompany its creation.

Crowning the apex of the castle rock, the memorial comprises a buttressed shrine protruding north from a 'U'-shaped gallery of honour. The latter is a remodelling of a disused barracks within whose ashlar-lined, rubble skin the nation's regiments are commemorated in spectacular sculpture and stained glass.

Ten years before its opening by the Prince of Wales, Lorimer had already supported the notion of a chapel built on the site, the style of which he asserted should be "of a sturdy, rather massive type of Scotch Gothic ... with external buttresses rising out of the rock". This early vision of indomitable strength weathered a media storm that the castle skyline would be disrupted, although the shrine – designed originally to be a freestanding octagon – was expressed in its third and final iteration as a chapel apse whose axial counterbalance was a shallow south-facing entrance porch with deep arched recess and diagonally-set gargoyles.

Rugged and rooted to its site (the ragged basalt emerging through the smooth granite floor), the building derives sophistication from the expertly proportioned interior and decorative work of the highest order. The stained glass is largely by Douglas Strachan, the sculpture, friezes and insignia chiefly by Pilkington Jackson and Morris and Alice Meredith Williams, the last of whom designed the figure of St Michael suspended from the ceiling. Carved roundels by Phyllis Bone pay tribute to the 'humble beasts' – including mice, donkeys, dogs and reindeer – all called innocently to service.

Union Bank of Scotland

St Vincent Street, Glasgow

James Miller

FEW ARCHITECTS CONVEYED the mercantile might of banking as powerfully as Miller. While his competition-winning design for the Union Bank owed much to transatlantic influences (in particular York and Sawyer's 1913 Guaranty Trust headquarters in New York), its antecedents were also found in Glasgow. So, it represented something of a natural progression in local architectural style.

Eight storeys high over a raised basement, built of pale polished ashlar on a slightly sloping corner site, the composition employs a giant order not once, but twice, reinforcing the importance of the institution. The Greek Ionic colonnade rising through the lower three floors on the entrance front (the massive bases at pedestrian head height) is flattened out in the form of pilasters on the Renfield Street façade, where the layout incorporated shops.

Higher, above an elaborate frieze and intermediate strip of small, evenly spaced windows, the second giant pilastrade corresponded to three floors of office accommodation. Above an attic storey of plain bipartite windows is a richly detailed entablature, its frieze studded with rosettes that act as a unifying decorative feature at various locations on the principal elevations.

The detailing may have been classical (or, more properly, neo-classical), but modernity demanded the use of metal-framed windows and spandrel panels filling the voids between the piers and pilasters, and white glazed brick on the rear wall. Construction was slowed (as was also the case at the Scottish National War Memorial) by the General Strike of 1926. The marble-lined, top-lit banking hall eventually opened its doors for business in November 1927. The building has since been re-modelled as lettable office accommodation.

North British and Mercantile Building

St Vincent Street, Glasgow

Sir John James Burnet of Burnet, Son and Dick

DARINGLY STRIPPED OF applied decoration, this monumental ashlar cube on a corner site represents Burnet's last major design. It has a purity and control that speaks of an architect embracing modernity with confidence and effortless ease: most of the deeply recessed windows have neither cill nor hoodmould, although some have the barest hint of keystone.

Detail is concentrated close to ground level, where on the entrance front to St Vincent Street there is a symmetrical arrangement of double-height arched windows separated by twinned Doric columns. The upper level windows are Diocletian in style and separated from the ground floor openings by deep recessed bands with exaggerated keystones. The remaining five tiers of windows are modestly proportioned, ten at each level on both south and west façades, the attic floor openings recessed beneath stepping, shouldered lintels. Two huge wallhead chimneys interrupt the eaves cornice on the principal corners: below one of these a large winged cartouche bears the entwined initials of the client.

For all its severity, there is nonetheless a designed sculpture scheme with maritime overtones. Flanking the main entrance are columns, their bases carved with stylised seahorses and their capitals a Viking longboat and galleon. Two heraldic shields adorn the lintel carried by these columns. Archibald Dawson's 1927 sculpture of St Andrew, standing in the prow of a ship, is at first floor level.

Completing the scheme in 1953, two magnificent crouching figures depict a seafarer and his wife, on the pedestal caps atop the principal pilasters. Their delayed appearance is thought to have been caused by shortage of funds. After all, the letters 'IOU' appear on the galleon's sail, the initial 'I' subtly disguised as a mast.

St Conan's Kirk

Loch Awe, Argyll

Walter Douglas Campbell

ALONG WITH HIS SISTER HELEN, amateur architect Campbell devoted the latter part of his life to this most exquisite of lochside buildings, ostensibly to relieve his mother of the lengthy trip to the church at Dalmally. In the event, he died before its completion. His legacy is an extraordinary, eclectic church of considerable charm in whose nave was incorporated the first kirk, a modest cruciform affair, completed in 1886.

Emboldened by this achievement, Campbell began work on an extended building in 1907, with the boulders for the walling rolled down from the hillside and split and shaped on site.

The approach from the road provides few clues to the originality of the loch-facing frontage or interior richness. First sight from the east is the broad, five-sided, parapet-topped, chancel ambulatory and entrance tower. These ill prepare the visitor for the splendour within, so a more rewarding route is first through the tiny cloister garth, with its decorative lead roofing, and then through the Norman archway to the south aisle.

Facing Loch Awe, the building is at its most scenic. Walls are heavily buttressed to accommodate the falling ground, the buttresses doubling as rainwater channels with boldly projecting gargoyles above. Where not fashioned in stone, the gargoyles are formed in lead – one set beautifully depicts a hound pursuing two hares. Above the south aisle a perfect pierced parapet is supported on a row of tiny carved owls.

Campbell was an enthusiastic antiquarian, and so architectural salvage (both actual and intellectual) abounds. There is a large window from the fifteenth century St Mary's Church in Leith, and weathered stonework from Iona Abbey is housed in a small recess.

St Conan's Kirk
© Crown Copyright: Historic Environment Scotland.
Licensor canmore.org.uk

India Tyre and Rubber Factory

Greenock Road, Inchinnan
Wallis, Gilbert and Partners

ARRESTING AND EXOTIC, the 1928 Firestone Tyre Factory on Brentford's Great West Road provided the template for the India Tyre Company's equally stunning Renfrewshire facility. The younger building was less ornate, but its Art Deco exterior shared the giant chamfered piers, stocky raised end pylons with stylised corbels, and glorious use of coloured glazed tile. It was a remarkable sight, even on the outskirts of a village built around airship manufacture.

Closed in 1922, the airship station had occupied a 413-acre site, and was undergoing redevelopment by India Tyres (who retained one large hangar) before the new Greenock Road office block was commissioned. Two storeys, originally fifteen bays long, symmetrically arranged around a tile-trimmed entrance portal, the building was constructed of reinforced concrete finished in dazzling white stucco.

Window bays were recessed (the windows metal-framed, originally chevron glazed), and separated at first-floor level by ribbed panels with a single green stripe. The stepped, fluted parapet centred on the principal front was proudly emblazoned 'India of Inchinnan' in italic script. Black, red and green tiles were used in controlled decoration, gold bringing luxury to the banded entrance architrave. Additions to either side around 1955 respected the original aesthetic, underlined by blocky pylon-like gatepiers and low roadside walls with simple geometric iron railings.

So much more than the 'country cousin' of the same firm's Hoover Building in West London, the Inchinnan office block is an important survivor. Reduced to a shell by the 1980s, it looked set to suffer the same fate as the demolished Firestone factory, but has since been renovated and revitalised as the headquarters of a telecommunications company.

India of Inchinnan

Scottish Legal Life Assurance Society Offices

Bothwell Street, Glasgow

Wright and Wylie

BELONGING TO THE BEGINNING of a decade during which classicism was surrendered slowly on the streets of Glasgow's insurance quarter, this urban behemoth was won in open competition in 1927. Later in life, architect Edward Grigg Wylie would spearhead the development of Scotland's modern industrial estates, but this building far more closely evidences the influence of his one-time employer Sir JJ Burnet.

Surrendering his post as Head of the Glasgow School of Architecture in 1921 in order to expand his practice, Wylie built nothing larger than the Bothwell Street offices. While none of the component parts of granite plinth, giant order, metal-framed windows and heavy cornice were unfamiliar in the city, they are here assembled with formidable rigour.

On plan, the building is an inverted 'U', the main frontage eight storeys high and facing north. Steel-framed, faced in pale Blaxter sandstone, the three principal elevations are expressed in picture-frame format – rusticated base, attic and entablature and corner 'towers' with quoins and punched-in openings. Occupying the centre, Corinthian pilastrades – four storeys in height – create alternating bands of dark and light, window and wall.

Corresponding to the floor levels are metal friezes cast with motifs depicting lions, horses and stylised thistles. This Moderne detailing is reinforced along Bothwell Street in the form of four superb Art Deco figurative panels at first floor representing Industry, Prudence, Thrift and Courage, carved in shallow relief by Archibald Dawson and James A Young. A more conventional, gilded, coat-of-arms surmounts the central of three entrance archways, while the shop frontages (framed in bronze) are amongst the most stylish in the city.

Scottish Legal Life Assurance Society Offices

ABOVE

© Jon Jardine

TERMS TERRACE

© Crown Copyright: Historic Environment Scotland. Licensor canmore.org.uk

St Anne's RC Church

Whitevale Street, Glasgow
Gillespie, Kidd and Coia

SO MUCH IS INNOVATIVE about this large cruciform church: the use of humble brick, for instance, then finding favour in Europe as a finishing material, but hitherto alien on the sandstone-lined streets of Dennistoun. This was the young Jack Antonio Coia's first commission for the Archdiocese of Glasgow, a client served faithfully for many years by architect Peter Paul Pugin, whose superb basilican-plan churches catered to catholic communities in architecturally unrivalled fashion, until Coia came along and picked up the mantle.

So, with a gradual shift in the established ritual of worship came changes in construction – a concrete frame, and red facing brick. Changes in plan-form generated a barrel-vaulted nave and sanctuary with stubby transepts, and arcades rather than aisles, all with unencumbered views of the altar. Finally, the style departed from the traditional with an Italianate frontage flattened and broadened, given brick and ashlar earlobes, a split pediment, a triple-arched entrance (carved with Celtic interlacing motifs) and flanking façades with barrel-headed windows, breaking the eaves of mansard roofs.

The design demanded exceptional craftsmanship; radial brickwork inside and out, cream sandstone exquisitely carved and decorative wrought-iron gates. Oak and smooth plaster brings light and life to the interior. The sculpture was by Archibald Dawson (the Madonna and Child keystone above the central entrance is especially fine), and the pediment is broken at its apex by a sturdy crucifix with a figure of Christ in partial relief.

The architectural themes tested in St Anne's were further developed in churches at Maryhill, Greenock and Rutherglen. Taken together, their influence would extend across the country and continue to shape new church architecture well after the Second World War.

St Anne's RC Church
© Jon Jardine

The Lane House
© Grant Bulloch

The Lane House
© Grant Bulloch

The Lane House

Dick Place, Edinburgh

Sir William Kininmonth with Sir Basil Spence

STUDYING TOGETHER AT Edinburgh College of Art, Kininmonth and Spence both joined the office of Rowand Anderson and Paul as young graduates: Kininmonth was offered a post first, declining unless Spence was allowed to accompany him. The two shared a salary and drawing board, splitting their time between salaried and self-employment so that they could work on a range of commissions. This creative liaison produced a series of striking modernist houses, including Kininmonth's own, built in the grounds of Frederick T Pilkington's 1865 mansion, Egremont.

Kininmonth would remark that opportunities to work in the 'modern' style were not afforded him initially. Admitting to being "more or less converted by Corbusier" by 1930, he rejected tradition in favour of the International Style when designing the family home. After all, what better client to work for, and what better way to promote his fledgling practice?

Later extended to the rear, the original concept was a single-storey cylinder (more properly an apse, containing the open-plan drawing room) extruded from the re-entrant angle of a two-storey 'L'- shaped block. Flat-roofed (a paved terrace above the drawing room), the house is built of brick, first painted white, but later harled. The bowed front of the drawing room is expressed as a continuous flush window wall looking over the garden (itself terraced). A concrete pergola leads to the garage.

Streamlined and sophisticated, the house was at first heated only by the single coal fire in the drawing room, the flue rising elegantly through the roof as a single *pilotis* supporting a cantilevered curved-end canopy sheltering a set of French windows. Kininmonth never moved house.

Tongland Power Station

Near Kirkcudbright, Dumfries and Galloway

Sir Alexander Gibb and Partners (Engineers)

IN ADDITION TO THE PRODUCTION of renewable energy, the 1929 Galloway hydro-electric scheme gifted to southwest Scotland industrial architecture of real refinement. Five generating stations, five reservoirs, a single barrage and a series of dams and tunnels, together delivered total peak power of around 106 megawatts.

Great efforts were made to reduce the impact of the development on the scenic beauty of Kirkcudbrightshire, Loch Doon Castle being dismantled from its island site and re-built to enable the loch to be used as the most northerly catchment. The dams were constructed in concrete, some with stylised parapets, huge sluice gates, all with fish ladders.

The power station at Tongland, largest of the five, its turbine hall appearing to float over the River Dee, came into operation first, in March 1935, acting as the control centre for this pioneering technological initiative. The scheme represented collaboration between electrical engineers Merz and McLellan and consulting engineer Alexander Gibb, responsible for the classical modern(e) style.

Tongland has a timeless quality, piers of cream-painted reinforced concrete alternating with ribbon strips of metal-framed glazing. There is a touch of Art Deco about the entrance, the eaves are recessed, and the tower linking the offices and turbine hall is a stylish pylon. Motive power (literally) drives the aesthetic, and so where the composition makes the greatest impact is in the beautification of the surge tank. This great banded and riveted steel chamber sits on a concrete arcaded rotunda, and even has a cornice. Designed to contain the pipeline water in the event of station shutdown, it protects the turbines from damage, but additionally acts as a prominent and dynamic landmark between road and river.

49

Commercial Bank of Scotland

Bothwell Street, Glasgow

James Miller

Commercial Bank of Scotland
© Crown Copyright: Historic Environment Scotland.
Licensor canmore.org.uk

THE LEAST CONVENTIONALLY classical of Miller's commercial buildings, conveying great size while relatively small: monochrome and audacious. Its one concession to its Victorian neighbour is to pick up the line of the adjoining balustrade in the dentilled string course. Turned on its head, this little bank would bend fewer rules, for the weight is carried at the top and the voids increase closer to the ground.

The largest of the openings is a deep cleft in the frontage facing Bothwell Street. Two three-storey fluted Corinthian columns manfully support the office floors above. Beyond the dazzling whiteness of the Portland stone walls, there is nothing light about this purposeful box. Even the frieze (a series of allegorical relief panels separating a row of square windows) commends Commerce, Justice and Prudence, albeit sculptor Gilbert Bayes was permitted to also celebrate Wisdom and Contentment.

That the roofline has no cornice, just a simple scroll, underlines an ongoing development in the architect's style. Nearing the end of his long career by the time the building was opened, he could be forgiven for reverting to type. Instead, he appears to have embraced an almost industrial aesthetic, the entrance sufficiently awe-inspiring to reassure customers of the power of the institution, and the exterior just decorative enough not to scare them away. Once inside, the thrifty were treated to a decorative scheme by Scott Morton and Company.

Surprisingly, the building has its origins in the northeast. It is, in fact, an extruded, refined version of Jenkins and Marr's 1929 Commercial Bank in Aberdeen, modified to suit a corner site. Inspiration closer to home than from across the Atlantic, given a gutsy Glaswegian twist.

Commercial Bank of Scotland

TOP LEFT

© Fiona Sinclair

TOP RIGHT, BOTTOM

© Jean O'Reilly

Neil Baxter HON FRIAS

SINCE MARCH 2008 Neil has been Secretary & Treasurer of The Royal Incorporation of Architects in Scotland (RIAS). Previously principal of his own consultancy and Development Director of the Glasgow Building Presentation Trust, Neil has lectured widely on architectural history and urbanism and written for *The Telegraph, Herald, Sunday Herald, Homes & Interiors* and *Architects Journal.*

As CEO, Neil is responsible for RIAS policy, governance, business planning and budgets. He also has oversight of the Incorporation's membership services, consultancy, practice services, accreditation, events, publications, outreach, political liaison, continuing professional development, educational initiatives and awards. At his job interview for the RIAS in December 2007 Neil proposed that, to mark its centenary in 2016, the Incorporation should organise a year long Festival of Architecture.

1936-1945

ESSAYS BY NEIL BAXTER HON FRIAS

Daily Express Building

Daily Express Building

Albion Street, Glasgow

Sir E Owen Williams

IN TIMES PAST, WHEN A daily paper was a necessity for most households, this huge, sleek monolith was effectively a great machine for producing newspapers. The raw material, giant rolls of newsprint, was offloaded in the ground floor loading bay at the front. Journalists and editors occupied the offices above and the block to the rear.

Behind the loading bay were the huge printing presses which, for over half a century, churned out hundreds of millions of copies, first of the mighty *Daily Express*, and latterly the *Glasgow Herald*, the longest running national newspaper in the world. The whole building shuddered when the great presses thundered into life.

Owen Williams had previously designed the *Express* headquarters in London's Fleet Street. The Glasgow building followed this example. Giant concrete cantilevers provided covered access for the trucks that delivered the raw paper and collected the finished product. Above the very functional ground floor, the whole of the building's façade was metal-framed ribbon glazing, a sheer striated surface of black Vitrolite concealing floor levels, with clear glazing to flood the building's floors with light.

Although amended over time with a rooftop extension and the glazing-in of the loading bays (when the building was converted to apartments) Owen Williams' building is still powerfully evocative of the great days of newspapers, when media moguls held great power. That power arose from the presses they controlled, but was also communicated through the buildings they commissioned. The sheer scale of the Albion Street building is impressive. But this was also a work of glamorous modernity, as elegant as it was huge, a veritable cathedral to the newspaper.

St Cuthbert's Co-operative Association

St Cuthbert's Co-operative Association

Bread Street, Edinburgh

T Waller Marwick

WHILE THE REST OF THE Co-operative building on Bread Street is stone-built and very traditional, the new infill block of the late 1930s was a revelation. Inspired by continental modernism, the glass façade was visibly separated from the structural concrete box, with its floor levels set behind.

The first time a glass 'curtain wall' was employed in the United Kingdom was at Bexhill-on-Sea. Erich Mendelsohn and Serge Chermayeff had won the early 1930s competition for a new seaside pavilion. What they created was crisp, sinuous, contemporary and got into all the papers. The judge of that competition was the Paisley-born, London-based architect, Thomas Tait.

According to contemporary sources, the architects in Marwick's office responsible for designing the Bread Street building were David Harvey, known as 'Speedy' and Philip McManus. However, at the same time as the Co-op was commissioning this building, Marwick was working alongside Tait on the Glasgow Empire Exhibition of 1938. Marwick, therefore, knew of the Bexhill building, not only from the architectural press but through the enthusiasm of Tait himself.

Although the frontage at Bread Street is narrow, the plan was deep with the wedge-shaped entrance drawing visitors one-third of the way into the building, past a lavish display of the goods that were available within. Similarly bold was the giant sign stretched across the whole façade, in letters two feet high.

Above the entrance, a patterned wall of glass on a widely-spaced structural frame 'hung' clear of the structural concrete beams and floorplates behind. This curtain wall was unlike anything previously seen in Scotland: there had never been a bolder retail building in Edinburgh.

St Columba of Iona RC Church

St Columba of Iona RC Church

Hopehill Road, Glasgow

Gillespie, Kidd and Coia

ONE OF A NUMBER OF remarkable 1930s churches by Jack Coia, this one came with the (not unusual) client demands that it should be simultaneously very large and built on a tight budget. Coia achieved the required scale and cost savings by using a concrete portal frame construction, fronted by an enormous oblong block.

On approaching the church, it is the giant brick screen of the entrance, flanked by two curved lower wings – on one side the baptistery, on the other enclosing the main staircase – that first impresses. While the overall effect is very much of its era, and not entirely dissimilar to some contemporary cinema architecture,

the inspiration for the detailing of the giant frontage is Italian Romanesque. A tall glazed cross is flanked by arcaded panels, whose triple arches are echoed in the stone-framed main entrance, itself surmounted by a carving of a bishop with a lamb, attended by angels.

The nave benefits from the full-height drama of the expressed structural frame. Light from the high clerestory windows bathes the interior. As with so much of Jack Coia's work, his appreciation of the creativity of others is evident in the painted stations of the cross by Hugh Adam Crawford, brought from Coia's Roman Catholic pavilion at the Glasgow Empire Exhibition, in late 1938, and the carved crucifix by the sculptor (and another great friend of the architect) Benno Schotz.

Unlike the rest of the composition, with its raw brick and concrete, the sanctuary, perhaps as a mark of its liturgical significance, is finished with plaster. Light floods from the side windows onto the elegant, marble altarpiece.

Luma Lightbulb Factory
© Keith Hunter

Luma Lightbulb Factory

Shieldhall Road, Glasgow

Cornelius Armour

THE SCOTTISH CO-OPERATIVE Wholesale Society, like so many large organisations of the time, had its own in-house architect. Perhaps because this building was about a very contemporary function, but also acknowledging its highly visible site, they gave their architect his head here to create something ultra-modern. It has been noted that this building, very Scandinavian in its inspiration, was not unlike contemporary airport buildings, complete with its glazed 'conning tower' – in fact, a highly visible testing bay for the product that was manufactured within. Its proximity to the Abbotsinch airstrip was perhaps no coincidence.

In 1930 the Stockholm Exhibition had helped establish modernist functionalism as the predominant architectural style, not only for Sweden but for much of continental Europe. The exhibition's chief architects, Gunnar Asplund and Sigurd Lewerentz, created buildings with exposed frames, large expanses of glass and crisp white exteriors. It took a while, but this style truly arrived in Glasgow with the Luma Building.

The Luma factory is a simple, three-storey, concrete structure with large glazing to draw in as much daylight as possible. Starkly plain, it would have been a very cost-effective solution, doubtless

a further strong argument which its architect would have used to persuade his bosses in the SCWS. From the very outset, however, it will have served as both factory and advertisement, promoting the light bulbs manufactured within and their technical innovation. This role, as a built advertisement, continued in the building's subsequent incarnation as a caravan saleroom. Thankfully, after a period of lying derelict, this elegantly plain, white-style, modernist factory has been lovingly restored and now serves as comfortable and very well-lit apartments.

Rothesay Pavilion

Argyle Street, Rothesay, Isle of Bute

J & JA Carrick

THIS 1936 COMPETITION-WINNING design gave Glasgow holidaymakers at the end of the 1930s an experience of stylish, modern seaside elegance to rival anything in Europe. Seaside pavilions were much in vogue in the 1930s, reflecting the increasing numbers of people who could afford a summer break. In Glasgow's case, for many holidaymakers, their nearest resorts were reached by train or steamer 'doon the watter' on the Clyde coast, and of course on the Isle of Bute, at Rothesay.

The main bulk of the building is the rectangular dancehall and auditorium, both in their heyday extensively programmed with seasonal light entertainment and very popular. Of course, for those who could afford the extra treat of dining out, the huge, glazed, cantilevered, semi-circular buffet was ideal. Above the buffet is an open-air roof terrace, pragmatically (this was still Scotland's west coast after all) covered by an over-sailing concrete canopy.

There is much in the Rothesay building reminiscent of the Bexhill-on-Sea Pavilion, another competition winner from earlier in the decade. Bexhill was designed by émigré architects, Erich Mendelsohn and Serge Chermayeff. The competition for this ultra-modern structure had been an architectural cause célèbre, marked by illustrated articles in both the professional journals and architectural press, and also many newspapers.

While James Carrick undoubtedly looked to Bexhill for inspiration – and his extensive glazing and the curved-end section might have been direct lifts from this English south coast precedent – his building was not quite in the same league in terms of architectural innovation. However, in its introduction of continental glamour to Rothesay, Mr Carrick's superb pavilion created something of truly international style and panache.

Rothesay Pavilion
© Crown Copyright: Historic Environment Scotland.
Licensor canmore.org.uk

St Andrew's House

Regent Road, Edinburgh

Burnet, Tait and Lorne

THE SITE FOR THIS BUILDING was formerly that of Edinburgh's Calton Jail. Its prominence seems thoroughly appropriate for Scotland's most important public building of the 1930s. An earlier proposal, for Government offices and the national library, outraged the public who considered the design lumpen and inappropriate for such a highly visible location.

The Royal Incorporation of Architects in Scotland, supported by The Cockburn Association, The Royal Fine Art Commission and Edinburgh Corporation, lobbied for a competition. The Government staged a limited selection process and the London-based Scot, Thomas Smith Tait, was declared the winner.

The building Tait designed for Regent Road is powerful and monumental. Two long wings extend from a square central block, each terminated by elegant, flat-topped, stair towers.

The influences on this building are many. The historian Charles McKean likened it to a giant Art Deco clock. The stair towers owe something to German modernism of the 1910s. The Dutch

St Andrew's House
© Grant Bulloch

architect, WM Dudok's influence has been detected in the blue tiled window details to the rear. Tait's office employed several Americans and the influence of Raymond Hood's New York giant Rockefeller complex is strong. It has also been suggested that the flat, overhanging roofs to the stair towers were inspired by another great American architect, Frank Lloyd Wright.

Irrespective of its architectural parentage, this is an impressively elegant building. Its north-facing front rises in height towards the pillared entrance with its magnificent bronze doors. The centrepiece of the great front elevation is an enormous carving of the royal coat of arms of Scotland. What began badly at the start of the decade, ended triumphantly in 1939 and endures as a celebration of Scots creativity and nationhood.

Glasgow Film Theatre

Rose Street, Glasgow

WJ Anderson II of John McKissack & Sons

THE COSMO WAS THE 'art' cinema in George Singleton's extensive Glasgow chain. Singleton was an impressive entrepreneur. Through his lifetime he built up one major chain of cinemas then sold that off before building up another. Glasgow's appetite for films in the 1930s was voracious, and the fact that the Cosmo was special was recognised from the outset. It has retained its place in the affections of Glaswegians and is still the venue for short runs, international film, limited release movies and the esoteric, right up to its present incarnation as the three-auditorium GFT.

The influences on this building were several. In the early thirties, the United Kingdom's first arthouse cinema was the Curzon in London's Mayfair, by the Paisley-born Thomas Smith Tait of the great London firm of Burnet, Tait and Lorne. To mark out his cinema as special and 'arty', Tait, instead of adopting the established approach to cinema design

of a lavish and fanciful façade, created something much more subtle.

At the Curzon, Tait's inspiration was partly Scandinavian, but mainly from the city architect of Hilversum in the Netherlands, WM Dudok. Dudok was an innovative modernist but his work was built in brick rather than concrete, and the brown brick-built GFT follows his and the Curzon's example. The design is made up of linear, long-stepped masses emphasised by long strips of faience (glazed terracotta) culminating in the stepped tower, rising above the entrance. The cinema's international focus was demonstrated by the great globe in the foyer.

Despite the large numbers of other cinemas that George Singleton commissioned, he was particularly associated, throughout his long life, with this one. He is still celebrated as 'Mr Cosmo', a fitting tribute!

Glasgow Film Theatre

The McMillan Reading Room, University of Glasgow

University Avenue, Glasgow

T Harold Hughes and DSR Waugh

VERY LITTLE ABOUT THIS building suggests its age. A concrete rotunda, faced in yellow brick, its form enabling maximum supervision with minimum staff, is set back within a generous site. Challenge anyone to guess its age and they are likely to suggest the 1960s rather than three decades earlier.

The reading stations are set on a radial layout with the central enquiries desk at the hub. This classical approach could have been inspired by any number of examples. Perhaps the best-known precedent in the United Kingdom was Sydney Smirke's 1857 Reading Room at the British Museum. Of course the original

inspiration for all such domed structures was the greatest surviving concrete building of the classical era, Rome's Pantheon.

In Glasgow, Hughes and Waugh created a building of rigid symmetry. The arch within the full-height, rectangular porch straddles a curving staircase. Vertical strip windows rise through the two-storey height of the building, regularly spaced around its circumference.

Hughes was Glasgow's Professor of Architecture from 1922 until his retirement, through ill health, in the early 1940s. As professor, he was first choice for a succession of university buildings.

His ambitions for the University estate were substantial: in 1938, he presented a masterplan for development around the three sides of the Reading Room, leaving the east side open, towards the magnificent Wellington Church. His plan also incorporated a square clock tower on an axial relationship with the tower of the main university building.

While his grand plan never came to pass, the Reading Room and much else Hughes designed for Glasgow University, stands in permanent memorial to one of its most inspiring and ambitious professors.

St Mary's Church of Scotland
© James Roy

St Mary's Church of Scotland
King Street, Aberdeen
A Marshall Mackenzie and Son

ST MARY'S CAME INTO BEING as the bringing together of several congregations. Commissioning Alexander (AGR) Mackenzie's practice was a sound move. He and partner John Gibb Marr rose to the challenge by creating an extraordinarily plain, supremely refined building. Although built in the local granite, as was the norm in the city, this is as modern as anything anywhere in Scotland at the time.

The affinities between this Aberdeen Church and what Jack Coia was building in Glasgow are strong. Just as with Coia's St Columba's RC Church in Maryhill, Mackenzie's practice created a fronting box tower with a simple portal frame construction behind. However, this design, in coursed snecked granite construction, has none of the layered façade detailing favoured by Coia. The tower entrance, nave and the connecting church hall, are a crisp composition of simple, abutted geometric forms, fully exploiting the precision of their granite construction. It has been said that this is one of the last all-granite buildings in Aberdeen.

Internally, the building is every bit as geometric and austere as its external form would suggest. Two low side-aisles flank an interior of almost monastic purity. White painted, with austere blonde wooden pews and furnishings, the whole seems little altered from its 1930s origins.

The nave is high, culminating in a very shallow pitched roof. As with the rest of the composition, the stained glass is elegant, its detailing simple and linear. The decorated window above the pulpit, centring upon the gaunt, attenuated figure of Christ, is superbly of its time. Like the whole of this masterly composition, this too is a simple, elegant, work of understated genius.

Bon Accord Baths
© Credit

Bon Accord Baths

Justice Mill Lane, Aberdeen
City Architects Department

IN ITS GRANITE MODERNITY, the exterior of this building is entirely appropriate to Aberdeen. The interior, on the other hand, conveys influences from much further afield. The giant concrete arches of the pool roof reflect leading-edge engineering from mainland Europe in the early years of the twentieth century. Meanwhile, the décor of the interior owes much to the Art Deco movement that began in Paris in 1925.

Working within the City Architects Department, but at a time when, fortunately and appropriately, local authority architects were given name checks, the architect, Alexander McRobbie, was intent on creating a new swimming pool for central Aberdeen which was as advanced as anything yet seen in Scotland.

The exterior is a great, buttressed, granite box. Once inside, the visitor was welcomed by blonde wood linings and shiny metal detailing. The Parisian *Exposition Des Arts Décoratifs* of 1925, which spawned its namesake movement, featured buildings that revelled in colour, bling and shiny geometries. Right up to the Second World War, Art Deco continued to declare glamour and international sophistication. At the Bon Accord Baths, the Deco style says, quite unequivocally, that nothing was too ritzy for the good citizens of Aberdeen.

McRobbie clearly enjoyed translating continental modernism into douce Aberdonian granite on the exterior and revelled in the decorative finishes of the interior. In the pool area itself the reinforced concrete roof structure followed on from continental industrial buildings of the 1910s (when the material was relatively new) and the elegance of the great bridges and innovative roofs of the brilliant Swiss civil engineer, Robert Maillart. This is arguably McRobbie's triumph – in a building that is one of Aberdeen's great hidden gems.

Euan Leitch

EUAN LEITCH IS THE Director of Built Environment Forum Scotland, an umbrella body for organisations with an interest in government policy on the historic environment. Previously, as the Assistant Director of the Cockburn Association (Edinburgh's Civic Trust), he coordinated Edinburgh's Doors Open Day and carried out conservation area appraisals as a freelance historic building consultant.

Edinburgh born, educated and resident, Euan studied Architectural History at the University of Edinburgh and Urban & Regional Planning at Heriot Watt University. Euan is in a long term relationship with the Architectural Heritage Society of Scotland where he has held a variety of roles. Euan has a particular interest in Scotland's post-war hydro-electric schemes and a soft spot for Brutalist buildings.

1946-1955

ESSAYS BY EUAN LEITCH

Timex Factory

Harrison Road, Dundee

Bennet, Beard and Wilkins

IN 1937 EDWARD GRIGG WYLIE of Wylie, Shanks & Wylie was appointed senior consulting architect to Scottish Industrial Estates Ltd to oversee the planning of industrial estates at Larkhall, Chapelhall, Newhouse, Queenslie and Dundee.

The Timex Factory (along with the nearby but now demolished National Cash Registers Factory) was designed in 1946 by the English architectural practice Bennet, Beard and Wilkins and typifies the factory design often employed on the Wylie estates. Long, low, flat-roofed and very simple it is predominantly yellow stock brick with the red sandstone entrance asymmetrically positioned at the east end. The windows form a continuous band, running off into the tree belt with a very subtle irregularity. The successful appearance of the Timex Factory owes much to its setting where it slices across the top of a gentle hill and it would be nice to attribute the drama to J Stanley Beard's background in cinema design.

The USA manufacturers were drawn to Dundee due to the then Lord Provost, Sir Garnet Wilson, actively responding to the Distribution of Industry Act in 1945. Timex employed around 7,000 at its peak, one of the principal employers in Dundee. The factory initially manufactured watches – it was the UK's largest supplier in the mid-1960s – then Polaroid cameras and the ZX Spectrum computer in 1983.

Timex finally closed their Dundee operations following a protracted and acrimonious industrial dispute in 1993. The Timex sign may be gone but the legacy of these early computer technicians and coders helped to give rise to Dundee's thriving gaming industry. The building is now home to a furniture manufacturer.

Timex Factory
© Jamie Howden

New Taybank Mill
© Jamie Howden

New Taybank Mill

Arbroath Road, Dundee

Kenneth Masson

TWO STOREYS OF RED BRICK with large steel framed windows, New Taybank Mill could have been a bright but basic factory. Designed by Kenneth Masson for the Scottish Co-operative Wholesale Society (SCWS) its details elevate it to a rather late Art Deco flower. The stacked porthole windows, *faience* (glazed terracotta) details and angled corner entrance with its floating, fluted and fluid columns suggest arrival at something more glamorous than the concrete-framed, steel-trussed jute mill that lay within. The corner site has two elevations, one sinking into the incline of Morgan Street.

Masson remained the Chief Architect for the SCWS until his retirement and this appears to be his most successful piece of new design. It is one of only two jute mills purpose-built in the twentieth century. Synonymous with Dundee, the jute industry began in the mid nineteenth century and employed 50,000 people by 1900, more women than men, across 130 mills in the city. The raw material – a natural fibre imported from what is now Bangladesh – was strong, durable, cheap, versatile and used to manufacture a wide range of products such as sacking, ropes, carpets, and sail cloth.

The industry was in decline by the mid twentieth century, and 'Juteopolis' finally fell when Tay Spinners closed New Taybank Mill in 1998 when the looms were dismantled and shipped to Kolkata, India. It was not just the last jute mill in Dundee but in the European Union. The interior spinning floors were subsequently demolished for a small housing scheme, leaving New Taybank Mill more a well conserved boundary wall than a building.

Wills Tobacco Factory
© Jean O'Reilly

Wills Tobacco Factory

Alexandra Parade, Glasgow

Wills Engineering Department

GLASGOW'S ARCHITECTURAL HERITAGE was enriched by the eighteenth century tobacco merchants' homes and warehouses. The Wills Tobacco Factory is a twentieth century tobacco industry equivalent. It was designed in-house by the Imperial Tobacco Company, a monumental quadrangle of red brick with contrasting stone details around the windows and doors.

The central entrance tower on Alexandra Parade, illuminated with three long vertical windows, contrasts with the four storeys of horizontal window bands on either side. The wings are book-ended by stair pavilions with cigarette slim windows. The building's style speaks of an earlier decade, post-war designers perhaps picking up from where they had left off before the Second World War.

There was a miniature version of the factory to the west, now demolished, where Wills manufactured cigars. At its peak the factory employed over 3,500 people. The next block was home to John Player's Tobacco (now artists' studios) and across the Parade was Gallaher's Tobacco – this was the smokiest corner of Dennistoun. Wills stopped manufacturing in Glasgow in 1992. Subsequently the building was converted to open plan office space with the addition of a glazed fifth floor and ubiquitous over-sailing eaves.

The Imperial Tobacco Company built a very similar, brick quadrangular factory for Wills Tobacco in Newcastle in the 1940s which closed in 1986 and was converted to flats in 1999. Imperial Tobacco also built a factory in Bristol in 1974, designed by the American architects Skidmore, Owings and Merrill which closed in 1990 and is currently (in 2016) being converted into flats. The legacy of the tobacco product may have been dark but the architecture of tobacco has found new life.

Vale of Leven Hospital

Alexandria, Dunbartonshire

Keppie Henderson and JL Gleave

THE FORMATION OF THE National Health Service in 1948 was the starter's pistol that resulted in the District General Hospital in the Vale of Leven being the first complete new-build hospital in Britain following the Second World War. The building programme required the possibility of expansion and the two-storey ward units were built to a modular pre-cast concrete system that permitted the addition of an extra floor.

The new NHS adopted a rationalist approach with small wards clustered around central service areas, a feature developed further in later hospitals. The concrete mullions separated glazing and panels of red cedar wood which follow an irregular pattern within the overall regular rhythm of the frame. The architects conducted extensive design research on the building system, the loss of traditional construction skills and shortage in bricklayers pushing them towards prefabricated methods that would go on to be used extensively in public sector construction in the following decades.

Even with the expected alterations and additions to a hospital over the last 60 years the original design remains visible and Ivor Dorward's 1968 maternity block continues the repetitive rhythm of the glazing, albeit over five storeys. The hospital is positioned within a landscape between the former gothic pile of Tullichewan Castle and Bromley House, both demolished in the twentieth century – historic landscapes frequently became home to modern institutions after the war.

The pursuit of the ideal building for health services continues in the nearby Vale Centre for Health and Care, completed in 2014 with a starfish plan. Like its much earlier Edinburgh predecessor, the Sighthill Health Centre, it draws various health services together but around a central atrium rather than a courtyard.

83

Fishermen's Houses

Lamer Street, Dunbar

Basil Spence and Partners

DUNBAR TOWN COUNCIL HAD commissioned Basil Spence and William Kininmonth to work on the regeneration of an area by Victoria Harbour in 1936. The result was a terrace of paired houses, stepping down the hill to the harbour, the most distinctive feature being an arch of grey tiles enclosing the front doors.

The second stage of the redevelopment found Spence and his partners working as confident modernists within the vernacular of Scotland's East Coast fishing villages. The modernist details of this post-war municipal housing development are found in the skinny iron railings, large windows and projecting concrete balconies while tradition continued with ground floor stores with forestairs, giving access to dwellings above, and the use of the distinctive, soft local red sandstone, clay pantiles and slate.

The informal groupings also provided the enclosure required for fishermen to dry and repair their nets, resulting in the picturesque qualities tourists expect of fishing villages. The scheme won a Saltire Housing Award in 1952, the successful combination of old and new resulting in Spence being given the commission for a similar approach at Newhaven, Edinburgh.

The architect Robert Hurd described the scheme as "an inspiring lead to other burghs" and sure enough it was emulated across Scotland by Wheeler and Sproson in Fife, Moira and Moira in Shetland and Robert Matthew in Cumnock. The scheme was included in the Dunbar Conservation Area in 1969. All that is missing today are some of the bright washes of colour Spence proposed: daffodil yellow, pale pink, pale blue, red and olive green, apparently incorporated to guide the fishermen back to their homes.

Fishermen's Houses

Extensions, Natural Philosophy Building

Extensions, Natural Philosophy Building, University of Glasgow

University Avenue, Glasgow

Basil Spence and Partners

THE NATURAL PHILOSOPHY building extension was a landmark in Scottish architecture. It provides the link between the pre-war and post-war approaches to modernism. It was for the internationally important research work of Professor Philip Dee, a leading figure in particle physics who played a key wartime role in developing airborne radar. Dee selected Spence to design the building that would house the 300 million watt Synchrotron which generated gamma rays to allow the study of matter at an atomic scale.

The basement is clad in traditionally finished Northumberland sandstone while the upper floors are clad in white Portland stone: tradition supporting the white heat of modernity. The flat roofs were finished in copper and the windows large and aluminium framed. The sculpted column at the entrance is a direct reference to the hugely influential Swiss architect, Le Corbusier and the cantilevered, wedge-shaped lecture theatre of the second phase informed by the Festival of Britain on the South Bank, London where Spence was also working.

The interior was just as striking. The mono-beamed staircase is a particularly sculptural feature and Spence's office designed the details from the tea bar and oak plywood panelling to laboratory doors and conference tables, light fittings and flower boxes. Unsurprisingly the estimated costs grew from an initial £140,000 to £400,000. Some of the residents in nearby Professors' Square did not welcome the visible arrival of the atomic age within the Gothic precincts of the university. They were disturbed not only by what they saw as an intrusion to the amenity of the university but by the fear of radioactive contamination. Happily the 150-ton sliding containment slab roof kept them safe from harm.

Sighthill Health Centre

Calder Road, Edinburgh

R Gardner-Medwin

ROBERT GARDNER-MEDWIN was appointed the Chief Architect and Planning Officer for the Department of Health for Scotland in 1947. His design for the Sighthill Health Centre was the first of its kind, a ground-breaking combination of health services around a welcoming courtyard plan.

Three sides of the courtyard are single storey, beneath very shallow pitched roofs. The windows form a continuous band above a brick base which is interrupted by three, timber-clad, window bays. The fourth side is two storeys over a basement with each level treated with a different cladding material: stone, brick and render. The highlight of the north elevation is a large glazed window, the full height of the building, which reveals an incredibly elegant, concrete spiral staircase with a 'Z'-shaped step profile.

The top floor dental surgeries have jutting, geometric window bays. The building has columns that once formed

sheltered areas to wait at two entrances, characteristic of the period. These have since been infilled, as has the generous courtyard within. The bright green copper roofs have been replaced by felt but the building still serves its original purpose as a local health centre.

An interesting comparison can be made with the Heilsuverndarstöðin in Reykjavik, another early 1950s health building with similar design moves – columns, elegant staircase and almost identical jutting geometric bay windows – albeit on a larger and more exuberant scale. Across Calder Road from the Sighthill Health Centre, is St Nicholas Church which was built around the same time, by Glasgow-based architects, Ross, Doak and Whitelaw. It too has a bright, colourful and fresh interior typical of the public buildings of the age in contrast to their institutional Victorian predecessors.

Sighthill Health Centre

ABOVE

© Charles McKean. Licensor www.scran.ac.uk

LEFT AND OPPOSITE PAGE

© Grant Bulloch

1954

Kilsyth Academy
Balmalloch, Kilsyth
Basil Spence and Partners

THE DESIGN AND CONSTRUCTION of Kilsyth Academy was interrupted and altered by global events and the founding of the post-war Welfare State. Spence designed it in 1930 when he was with Rowand Anderson Paul & Partners. Construction began in May 1939 but this was halted by the outbreak of the Second World War.

The Education Act of 1944 raised the school leaving age to 15 which would therefore result in a larger school roll and new regulations required every class to have its own classroom. It also became desirable for girls and boys to have separate halls for gymnastics. All this, combined with the addition of a swimming pool, increased the programme for the school building.

Building re-started in 1946 to an amended design from Spence's own practice, Basil Spence and Partners. The pre-war design bears much in common with contemporaries such as J&F Johnston's school designs for Ainslie Park

and Berwickshire High; long, two storey blocks around a courtyard and a light Art Deco spirit about the clock tower.

The amended, post-war, plans retained the layout but the school hall developed a boldly splayed plan – a nod to the Festival of Britain style – resulting in a striking building situated on a prominent hilltop. A sculptural relief representing Education, by the artist Tom Whalen, adorns the side of the clock tower.

As with the other public buildings of this period the school has been subject to alteration, albeit broadly sympathetic. The most significant change is an additional wing to the east that respects Spence's original design. The triple-eyed school hall forever gazes upon Kilsyth.

1955

NATIONAL LIBRARY OF SCOTLAND

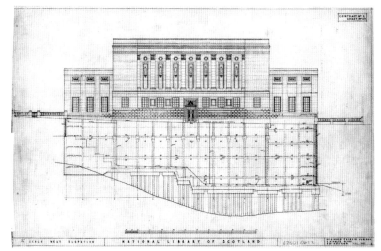

National Library of Scotland

George IV Bridge, Edinburgh

Reginald Fairlie (completed by AR Conlon)

THE NATIONAL LIBRARY OF SCOTLAND was constituted by an Act of Parliament in 1925, following the Advocates' Library being gifted to the nation. Sir Alexander Grant of Forres, creator of the original McVitie's Digestive Biscuit, donated £100,000 to the building of a new library and the Government matched his donation.

Construction began in 1937 to the architect Reginald Fairlie's design, only to be halted by the outbreak of war in 1939. Building resumed after the war. Fairlie died in 1952 and Alexander Conlon, a partner in his practice, took the building to completion. He appears to have made very minor revisions to Fairlie's design, simplifying the decorative capitals on the giant pilasters on the main elevation.

An interesting comparison can be made with Conlon's 1958 St Francis-Xavier RC Church in Falkirk where he worked with the same group of artists and shows his hand freed from Fairlie's particular rigour. A steel frame clad in fireproof concrete supports seven floors of library stacks below ground level with two airy floors above ground level. Clad in Blaxter stone, Fairlie himself described it as "frigid serenity".

A host of contemporary artists contributed to the external reliefs and the tall figures are by Hew Lorimer symbolising the arts of civilisation: Medicine, Science, History, The Poetic Muse, Justice, Theology and Music. The interior has a cinematic imperial staircase with a glass window etched with thistles and crowns by Helen Monro. The windowless reading room keeps out the noise from George IV Bridge but is top-lit by a series of circular cupolas. There are reported to be 50 miles of shelving containing over two million books.

Hermit's Castle
© Barnabas Calder

Hermit's Castle

Achmelvich, Loch Inver, Sutherland

David Scott

SCOTLAND'S COAST IS DOTTED with gun emplacements from the Second World War, poured concrete pillboxes that allowed servicemen to scour the horizon for enemy ships. They are now atmospheric relics, battered by winds and often providing shelter for sheep. The Hermit's Castle is their even more enigmatic architectural relative. Sitting high above a rocky inlet half a kilometre away from the nearest habitation, it is constructed from in-situ poured concrete and appears to grow from the rock it sits on, the cement presumably mixed with local sand and aggregate. The entrance is very narrow and sits on the cliff edge, facing out to sea. It contains one simple room with a bed platform, fireplace, concrete shelving, a high strip of small square windows and the ceiling is barely two metres high. It is a one-man castle.

It was built by a young architect, David Scott from Norwich, over one summer in the 1950s. The story goes that he was escaping from the pressure of family expectations and while he spent months carrying materials across the peninsula, upon completion he only slept in it once, never to return.

The remote cell-like nature, combined with the story of escape have no doubt given rise to the building's name. It lost its glazing and door in the 1970s and is now (in 2016) on the *Buildings at Risk Register* but it is still clearly in occasional use as a shelter. The Hermit's Castle could be seen as an Expressionist version of the Second

World War gun emplacements. There is scant verifiable fact about Scott or his motives for building his retreat. He died, in care, in Norwich in 2013.

Frank Walker OBE FRIAS

FRANK ARNEIL WALKER studied at the Glasgow School of Architecture. He has practised as an architect and for many years taught architectural design and architectural history at the University of Strathclyde where he obtained his doctorate. He is now Professor Emeritus.

Frank has written on a variety of topics such as Scottish Baronial architecture, the development of urban form in Scotland, fin-de-siecle architecture in Central Europe, and is the author or co-author of some 20 books including three volumes in the prestigious *Buildings of Scotland* series. Frank is author of *The Scottishness of Scottish Architecture*, due to be published in 2016 as part of the Festival of Architecture. He was appointed an OBE in 2002.

1956-1966

ESSAYS BY FRANK WALKER OBE FRIAS

The Townhouse
ABOVE
© Grant Bulloch
OPPOSITE PAGE, LEFT
© Grant Bulloch
OPPOSITE PAGE, RIGHT
© Courtesy of Historic Environment Scotland.
Licensor canmore.org.uk

The Townhouse

Wemyssfield, Kirkcaldy

David Carr of Carr and Howard

A COMPETITION-WINNING design of 1937. Building began in 1939 but was soon halted by the outbreak of war. Construction resumed in 1950 and the work was finally completed in two phases by 1956. Fronting a paved town square along its entire length, the principal west façade is three storeys high, the walls ashlar-faced, the regularly spaced windows tiered in neo-classical manner, the roof flat behind a corniced parapet.

Decorative detail is minimal with attention focused on the main entrance which is set, off-centre to the left. Here, steps rise to a single-storey, flat, copper-roofed porch above and behind which,

framed in plain pilasters and cornice, tripartite glazing lights the two upper floors. Rising from the roof, aligned with this entrance axis, is a thin belfry steeple and weather vane, its form clearly derived from Scandinavian precedent. Constructed in copper, this slender tower features a carving of St Bryce, patron saint of Kirkcaldy.

The plan of the building is straightforward. A long, three-storey, office block with a central corridor, runs north-south with a short return to the east at its south end. From the asymmetrically placed entrance a short wing extends east. In the main entrance hall, which is

galleried at the upper levels and top-lit behind the steeple, an imperial staircase rises to the council chamber at first-floor level. A secondary stepped approach enters the building axially from the end of the east wing.

The prolonged lapse of time between the building's design and its completion has resulted in an evident yet endearing anachronism; polite in detail, the building's tentative modernism is modified by a lingering classicism.

St Paul's RC Church

Warout Road, Glenrothes

Gillespie, Kidd and Coia

THE FIRST AND STILL ONE of the finest of a series of post-Second World War churches which the architects designed for the Roman Catholic Church in Scotland over a period of some 25 years. The plan is a symmetrical trapezium, the parallel sides of which are set at right angles to the liturgical axis.

From the shorter west wall, where the church is entered through a baptistery vestibule, the side walls splay outwards so that the nave is at its widest along the east wall. Abutting the centre of this east wall is a rectangular sanctuary reflecting the width of the entrance wall opposite. A tower capped with a slated monopitch roof and a cross rises over the sanctuary, its west wall glazed above the flat roof of the nave so that the high altar below is bathed in light – a strategy clearly inspired by the work of the Swiss modernist, Le Corbusier.

The glazing of the tower and the west entrance wall, both of which incorporate panels of coloured glass, is irregularly patterned in timber framing of thin verticals and broad horizontals. Walls are of white-painted loadbearing brickwork.

On the sanctuary wall is a crucifix, wrought in metal with biblical symbols and a pieta at the base; the work of sculptor Benno Schotz. A short glazed link connects the church entrance with low flat-roofed offices and presbytery, forming a 'U'-plan to the south-west.

Here and there the building is somewhat compromised by later failures to respect its minimalist aesthetic. However, though constructed to a tight budget, the building's spatial simplicity, its use of light and raw detailing are powerfully architectural.

High Sunderland

Galashiels, Scottish Borders

Peter Womersley

BUILT FOR THE TEXTILE DESIGNER Bernat Klein, this remarkable residence is located on a rise in woodland in the estate park of nineteenth century Sunderland Hall. The rectangular plan, defined by a modular grid of posts and beams, comprises four elements. Two parallel, partially overlapping, oblongs contain the accommodation; the larger, looking south, housing the principal living areas and master bedroom; the other, the guests' and children's bedrooms. A sheltered garden and pool lie in the re-entrant angle created by these two units while a double garage completes the overall plan on the north-west.

The white-painted timber structure is flat-roofed with some areas left open to the sky. Wall panels of timber lining, rubble stone, sliding windows, variegated glass and fabrics designed by Klein define internal and external spaces in a free disposition which offsets the austere geometry governing the plan. Given the spatial fluidity of the concept it is fortunate that the architect was able to design all the internal fixtures and furnishings. A special feature was Womersley's creation of a sunken living space set slightly below and open to the studio, library and dining room which surround it. Here, a fireplace rises at the very heart of the plan.

The planning of the house is clearly influenced by the work of the great German architect, Mies van der Rohe, though the sophisticated ascetic rigour of Mies's interiors has been shunned. In the horizontal lines of the nearby Studio which Womersley designed for Klein in 1970 the architect's debt is more to Frank Lloyd Wright, his use of poured concrete intimating a growing affection for more textural, even Brutalist, qualities.

Avisfield

Cramond Road, Edinburgh

Morris and Steedman

PERHAPS THE FIRST POST-Second World War private house built in Scotland to exemplify an intelligent and uncompromising grasp of twentieth century architectural ideas. Built within a limited budget on a relatively confined suburban site, this small but remarkably spacious home has a deceptively simple plan shaped by two interpenetrating flat-roofed rectangles.

A terraced living area, kitchen and bedroom enjoy views to the north while the 'L'-plan configuration embraces a south-facing garden court. The high-walled boundary, built in rubble stone, not only provides shelter and privacy from the busy road which passes the site on the south but is subtly articulated to set up formal relationships between the garden landscape and the house.

Centrally located in the overall plan, close to the inner angle of the courtyard, a large fireplace with hearth and inglenook is also constructed in rubble stonework. Beside this core an opening in the roof lets added light into the heart of the home. Sliding glass windows open to the sunny courtyard where the family can relax and children can play in safety.

Compact yet permeated by the rectilinear interplay of internal and external space defined by roof and wall planes, the house has a distinctly American flavour, its young designers, still in their final year of study at Edinburgh College of Art, already influenced by the published work of the hugely influential American architects, Frank Lloyd Wright, Richard Neutra and Rudolf Schindler. Further study in the United States confirmed them in this approach and bore fruit in a succession of outstanding private house commissions when they returned to Scotland.

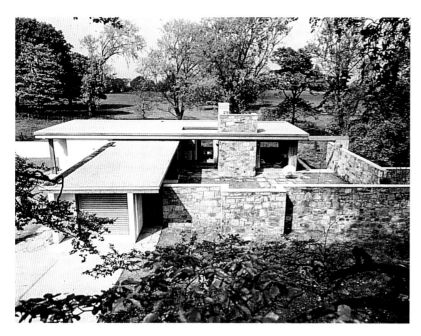

Silitto Residence

Charterhall Road, Blackford Hill, Edinburgh

Morris and Steedman

AN OUTSTANDING EXAMPLE of the architects' domestic design, one of a series of private houses built in the 1950s and 60s which set a new standard for residential architecture in Scotland. Built in an inner suburb of Edinburgh, the location is nevertheless almost rural. On an elevated site, approached diagonally from the north on a slow path stepping up the hillside, this chaste house makes a stunning architectural impact through the simplest of solid geometries.

A timber-framed rectangular box, glazed to the north and south to allow the full width of the upper-floor living space to take advantage of the views from Blackford Hill, advances slightly over a long white-rendered wall concealing the ground-floor accommodation. This lower wall, penetrated by a single entrance doorway, extends beyond the upper storey, particularly to the west where it returns to define a partly paved garden space open to the south.

Behind the wall, sheltered and private, ground-floor bedrooms open east and west onto small terraces. From the entrance, a straight-flight stair rises centrally to the upper floor where with the galley kitchen it forms an island core in the open-plan living space. The windowed walls north and south, glazed above continuous cill-height cupboard space, are regularly articulated by timber mullions, the east and west end walls timber-lined.

The whole conception has an austere elegance clearly a consequence of the architects' time in the United States where at the University of Philadelphia they had come under the influence of the American architect, Philip Johnson. The asceticism of the building's geometry and its exquisite relationship to the wider landscape, hint too at Japanese influence.

107

Seafar Housing

Cumbernauld New Town

Cumbernauld Development Corporation

BY THE LATE 1950S, government put a strong emphasis on slum clearance – millions were uprooted from cramped inner-city tenements. The 1960s saw a marked rise in the number of houses being built in Scotland by local authorities, the Scottish Special Housing Association and the New Town corporations. Some of the best New Town residential developments were in Cumbernauld. A number of satellite neighbourhoods of medium density low-rise housing were grouped, in carefully landscaped clusters, around the town's megastructural hill-top hub. Strict planning policies, devised to separate people and vehicles, ensured that residents could enjoy safe pedestrian access to the town's commercial and administrative centre.

Housing at Seafar, located to the north of the centre, on falling ground overlooking the Campsie Fells, was the second such neighbourhood to be built. At Seafar 1, designed by Roy Hunter

Seafar Housing

and Harry Causer, streets of two-storey terraces with monopitch roofs were constructed while at Seafar 2, by Roy Hunter and Harry Eccles, the terraces, some of which were in split-level arrangement exploiting the slope of the site to the north, were flat-roofed.

The architecture was reserved: the house plans simple; the building forms regular. Though modestly varied, with changes in ground level and the provision of entrance porches to the south, the use of materials – slated roof planes, rendered walls and some timber boarding was not without deference to Scottish tradition.

Despite the exposed nature of the site, the neighbourhood layout and the landscaping, which incorporated small courtyards connected by pedestrian ramps, afforded 'intimacy, privacy and shelter'. As a result, Seafar housing gained an Award of Distinction from the Saltire Society in 1961.

Gala Fairydean FC Stand

Nether Road, Galashiels

Peter Womersley and Ove Arup & Partners

A SMALL SMALL-TOWN spectator stand seating 750 people which, through the mutually beneficial and creative collaboration of architect and engineer, occasions unexpected delight. In cross section, two cast-concrete wedge-shaped forms – raked seating terrace and cantilevered canopy – seem to hinge precariously on a thin vertical edge. At the rear, along the length of the stand, four 'V'-sectioned vertical concrete fins buttress and complement this dynamic conjunction of forms.

Spectators sit on timber benches on the stepped concrete structure. Below, a low ground-floor storey houses a bar

and ancillary accommodation, though some later changes here compromise the building's original clarity. Raised over the turnstile entrances beyond each end of the stand, inverted concrete pyramids echo the sharp angularity of the canopy above.

At once sophisticated in form and rugged in finish, the building may be described, with complimentary rather than pejorative intent, as brutalist. Less provocatively categorised as a key work of late modernism, the stand's pronounced sculptural quality, coupled with its use of off-the-shutter boarded concrete, exemplifies a more modelled textural

approach to architectural design. From the 1960s, under the inventive influence of the Swiss modernist Le Corbusier's work from the previous decade, this began to supersede the white-walled rectilinearity so fashionable earlier in the century.

Yet this starkly angular, 'origami-like' composition of facetted planes has its more precocious forebears too. Perhaps most notably in the unique pre-First World War work created by the architects and designers of Czech (Prague) Cubism. That this relationship may not have been acknowledged by the designers does not diminish their achievement nor does it make the coincidence any less alluring.

Glasgow College of Building and Printing

LEFT
© Jon Jardine

ABOVE
© Crown Copyright Historic Environment Scotland.
Licensor canmore.org.uk

OPPOSITE PAGE
© Jean O'Reilly

Glasgow College of Building and Printing

North Hanover Street, Glasgow
Wylie, Shanks and Underwood

ONE OF THE EARLIEST high-rise non-residential buildings to be constructed in Glasgow and one of the most accomplished in Scotland, this multi-storey tower exploits its hillside site to dominate the city's George Square to the south. The plan, sometimes loosely described as 'coffin-shaped', more accurately takes the form of an elongated symmetrical lozenge, a configuration probably derived from the great Swiss modernist Le Corbusier's redevelopment proposals for Saint-Dié (1945-46) or perhaps his unsuccessful 1933 competition design for the Rentenanstalt Building in Zurich.

Six bays of raw concrete *pilotis* (free standing columns or stilts – another of Le Corbusier's innovations) carry a reinforced concrete frame 13 storeys high. A lower later block of accommodation from 1969, square in plan, advances north to Cathedral Street.

To the south, a dramatically cantilevered concrete *porte-cochère* canopy projects over the entrance. Above, the subtly canted wall planes of the north and south elevations are hung with curtain-wall glazing incorporating black vitrolite panels. On the west and east elevations, the blank gables are clad in travertine stone.

On the roof is an open terrace with gymnasium, plant rooms, penthouses, etc. expressed as strong sculptural shapes set against the skyline. This is yet another architectural gambit drawn from the work of Le Corbusier, whose Unité d'habitation projects, most notably in South Marseille, feature similar sculptural rooftop forms. The architect (Peter LA Williams) also designed the neighbouring Central College of Commerce and Distribution (1963), a building similar in concept though rectangular in plan and only seven storeys high. In both cases he produced stunning architectural perspective drawings of his designs, their glazed walls rendered "like a great looking glass [to] reflect the scudding clouds".

St Patrick's RC Church

Low Craigends, Kilsyth

Gillespie, Kidd and Coia

ONE OF A SERIES OF remarkable churches, radical in form and materials, designed by the architects in the 1950s and 60s for the Roman Catholic Church in Scotland. Walled in facing brick, essentially a high rectangular box, the public face of this church is austere but internal dignity and delight is generated by the imaginative modelling of light and shade.

The flat steel-framed roof with its deeply splayed copper-clad fascia appears to float over a continuous glazed clerestory. Natural lighting to the load-bearing brick diaphragm walls on each side of the nave is ingeniously contrived. On the south, over the confessionals, the light spills through tall windowed slots of differing widths and planes; on the north, above a long low gallery raised half a floor height above the nave, light enters from above in an irregular series of hollowed-out shafts.

At the west end of the gallery a raking rooflight falls over the baptistery while at the diagonally opposite corner of the plan the raised sanctuary is flooded with light from the south where a narrow wall of glass, hidden behind the Lady Altar, rises to a small monopitch rooflight.

The narrow gallery which, but for the top-lit baptistery at the west end, extends along the north side of the nave, is carried on fifteen parallel reinforced concrete barrel vaults. These are expressed both internally and on the north elevation where they advance to support the hollowed wall above. Below the gallery a semi-basement accommodates sacristy and mortuary chapel. A prolonged restoration, completed in 2000, has returned the church to its original form and finish.

St Patrick's RC Church
ABOVE TOP
© The Glasgow School of Art
ABOVE
© Andrew Lee
OPPOSITE PAGE
© Andrew Lee

St Peter's College

Carman Road, Cardross
Gillespie, Kidd and Coia

FROM THE THREE DECADES in which, guided by Jack Coia, Isi Metzstein and Andy MacMillan thrilled with a string of outstanding buildings, the seminary at Cardross, even in its current state of dereliction, stands as their shared masterpiece.

The great Swiss architect, Le Corbusier's Dominican monastery at La Tourette was undoubtedly an inspiration. While the direct borrowing of Corbusian features – the domed roughcast shells of the meeting cells, the light cannons, the orchestrated vertical rhythms of the window mullions and the rough pebble finish to the precast surrounds of the novices' sleeping cells – all pay homage

to the master, it would be quite mistaken to conclude that this had been a re-imagination of the contemporary French counterpart to St Peter's.

While further similarities to La Tourette exist in the manner in which the elements of the brief are set around a courtyard, each within its respective landscaped setting and with the sleeping cells oversailing the communal spaces on the top floors, the genius (and sheer audacity) of the architectural solution lay in the organisation of the section through the main building.

A bold megastructure was conceived, housing all of the functions of the seminary in a single block, exploiting the

opportunities for heightening the scale of the building on this gently sloping site and, at the same time, increasing the drama of the internal collegiate spaces. Illuminated by reflected light, this reinforced the sense that the student priests were part of a single, shared community.

Many years later, as the building struggled to secure new uses, Isi Metzstein reflected on its future. He indicated, with the directness and perception for which he is fondly remembered, that he could imagine St Peter's as a "beautiful ruin".

Andrew PK Wright OBE PPRIAS

ANDREW WRIGHT IS A Past President of The Royal Incorporation of Architects in Scotland, an accredited conservation architect and an architectural historian. He has served on many public bodies engaged in the care and promotion of the historic environment and has acted as conservation adviser to numerous building preservation trusts.

In collaboration with many of Scotland's leading architects, Andrew's work has often involved carrying out in-depth research into the history of a site and its development, leading to the preparation conservation plans and heritage reports – key documents that have guided the design process in the course of managing creative change. Among his current projects are buildings designed by Sir William Chambers, Thomas Hamilton, William Playfair, Charles Rennie Mackintosh, William Leiper, Sir Robert Lorimer, and Sir Ninian Comper.

1967-1975

ESSAYS BY ANDREW PK WRIGHT OBE PPRIAS

School of Architecture, University of Strathclyde

Rottenrow, Glasgow

Frank Fielden & Associates

STRATHCLYDE UNIVERSITY RECEIVED its charter in 1964, attracting Frank Fielden north to take up the post of its first Professor of Architecture. It is either a brave choice, or a foolhardy one, for a head of school to venture on designing a new building housing his or her own school of architecture. Expectations would have been high in this instance as this was the first post-war, purpose-designed, architecture school building to be erected in the UK.

The floor plans and elevations were derived directly from the spatial needs of the individual student, manifested in the form and height of the well-proportioned projecting bays to the studios at the first and second floor levels. The angled northlights on the skyline reinforce the rhythm of the studio bays, and direct light is further controlled through the use of copper-clad panels. Blue engineering brick is used extensively for the infill panels and across the plinth to the building shared with the slightly later Colville Building to the south but, overall, the palette of materials is restrained.

The studio floors oversail the ground floor giving shelter, and monotony is avoided by splaying the brick walls to the tutors' rooms. While the design is uncompromisingly of its time, it falls well short of the wilder excesses of the New Brutalism favoured by contemporary designers. When built, it commanded the Rottenrow ridge where it still sits comfortably, but its supremacy within the campus would be challenged almost instantly as it came to be dominated by new university department buildings of a lesser architectural quality, erected in accordance with the masterplan for the site prepared by Robert Matthew.

Mortonhall Crematorium

Howdenhall Road, Edinburgh

Basil Spence, Glover & Ferguson

SPENCE WAS ALREADY A household name as a consequence of rebuilding Coventry Cathedral when, in the year before Coventry was consecrated, he was awarded the commission for the Mortonhall Crematorium. By now the bulk of his time was spent in London, although the guiding hand throughout the evolution of the design was undoubtedly his.

The concept of the architectural space framing the celebrant (or in this case, the coffin) and the effect of diffused, coloured light passing through painted or stained glass to illuminate the plain internal wall surfaces, reveal the influence of Le Corbusier's pilgrimage chapel at Ronchamp. Setting the building in a clearing deep within the established woodland of the site allowed Spence to create a dignified, extended route for the bereaved, from the entry into the site to the point of arrival at the chapels. While this echoed the stunning achievement of Gunnar Asplund at the Woodland Cemetery in Stockholm, in many other respects the design has a timeless, Nordic appeal.

Materials are restrained, and are exquisitely detailed. Externally, the walls glisten from the reflection of light from the calcined flint aggregate masonry blocks, laid in alternating course heights, contrasting with the woodwork in a warm red cedar colour.

Spence's skill was in articulating the contemplative spaces from the angular walls on plan, using the basic building geometry to link the two chapels with the lower entrance block. The walls of the chapels extend upwards to provide a cluster of angled planes giving three-dimensional form to the plan. A pyramidal rooflight rises above the angled walls, contrived to cast a shaft of light on the coffin.

Nuffield Transplantation Surgery Unit, Western General Hospital

Crewe Road South, Edinburgh

Peter Womersley

THE WORLD'S FIRST BUILDING to be specifically designed for the transplantation of human organs, the plan is organised in three parts disposed on differing levels: sterilisation section, operating suite and patients' rooms. The complex services needed to provide a germ-free environment are cleverly integrated in plan and section with the building's reinforced concrete structure in a robust constructivist aggregation of horizontal and vertical elements.

Barrel-vaulted beams, which extend to the building's perimeter to carry deep concrete parapets, are coincident with the alignment of horizontal service runs while vertical ducts are expressed as separate structural shafts grouped in pairs rising above the flat roof of the bridge.

The sculptural quality of the building is further accentuated by the setting of some window and duct openings in swept curved frames which project from the wall planes. Overall, this forceful formal expression of services and structure is intensified by the choice of material

– ochre-coloured pre-cast concrete panelling and concrete cast in situ poured against fibreglass-lined formwork. The result is "an aesthetic of geometric, concrete monumentality" – one of Scotland's most robust essays in Brutalist architecture.

In the April 1968 issue of *Architectural Design* magazine, Edwin Johnston observed:

"Aesthetically the building is full of surprises. Restricted isolated areas of intense colour effectively applied invade quite restful spaces where the consistent muted browns of the internal concrete predominate. Artificial lighting is excellent and the exploration of its potential visual effects is typical of the immense care and thought applied elsewhere in the design. For example, in the stair tower, an ingenious strip light built into the balustrade throws light in the most appropriate place – also lending a subtle visual emphasis to the half cantilevered precast concrete treads."

Nuffield Transplantation Surgery Unit

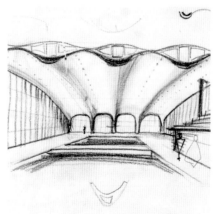

Dollan Aqua Centre

Off Brousterhill, East Kilbride
Alexander B Campbell

IN HIS FORMATIVE YEARS, Alexander Buchanan Campbell experienced the thrill of working on the first *Queen Elizabeth* in the drawing office of Cunard in Liverpool, but in many respects he typifies the sort of architect who rarely practises outside his own area, carrying out a corpus of distinguished work over a lifetime for the communities he served.

In the brief for the Dollan Baths Campbell seized the opportunity, on this hilltop site, of creating a building which, more than any other in East Kilbride, holds out the prospect of a futuristic vision from living in one of Scotland's new towns, even though the reality might have been different for some.

For this he looked abroad, to the Italian architect engineers who, since the 1930s, explored to the full the aesthetic boundaries of reinforced concrete engineering, finding ultimate expression in the post-war sports arena and exhibition halls. Inspired by the Palazetto dello Sport by Pier Luigi Nervi, designed for the Rome 1960 Olympics, the soaring 324ft parabolic arch is the *tour de force* of the bold composition, with the forces transmitted to the ground by bifurcated struts at a dauntingly shallow angle. So remarkable was Buchanan Campbell's achievement, it attracted professional visitations from home and abroad during construction.

This perennially popular venue was given a makeover in the mid-1990s, and again more recently. While this has diluted some of the quality of the original design, the distinctive structure has lost none of its power. It is seen best from the open parkland to the northeast of Brousterhill, the site having been selected with considerable care by the architect.

Andrew Melville Hall, University of St Andrews

Off Guardbridge Road, St Andrews

James Stirling

BORN IN GLASGOW IN 1926, James Stirling was, and remains for many, the ultimate 'architect's architect' and it is unfortunate that the halls of residence at St Andrew's University is his only built work in Scotland. It was the first major commission to be undertaken after his professional split with James Gowan.

Stirling's architectural approach was innovative, iconoclastic and often controversial, but it was always highly influential. He was commissioned by the university to design a masterplan for the site, set beyond the historic burgh on ground falling away below a cliff-top walk and with open views to the sea. However, in the uncertain economic climate to which the funding of higher education was subjected at the time, only one of the four planned units was built of what would have resulted in a self-contained settlement of 1,000 students.

The rational interplay of powerful geometry of the plan and three-dimensional forms of the much admired 1963 Leicester Engineering building are at play here, with the projecting window bays of the rooms angled to take advantage of the views of the seascape. Stirling conceived the building so that the height and bulk of the splayed residential wings were disguised on the approach from the cliff walk.

The unifying element in the whole design is the horizontal walkway with the architect's trademark patent glazing, running around the three sides of the internal court at the mid-point of the residential wings. This provides the primary circulation linking the wings with the fully glazed central block. It was also conceived to encourage socialising among the students. The wings step down, following the slope of the land.

BOAC Building

Buchanan Street, Glasgow

Gillespie, Kidd and Coia

OCCUPYING A NARROW corner plot on Glasgow's premier shopping street, and erected as offices and a showroom for the corporate airline giant BOAC, this commercial project may seem at first an unusual commission for the architects to be awarded. Effectively, their response was to reinterpret the traditional nineteenth century street frontages of the neighbouring properties in a modern idiom.

Each of the elements of the composition is articulated from the others, consisting of a plinth, incorporating the showroom windows at street level; the superstructure of three regular storeys accommodating the offices; and above that, a floating band replacing the traditional cornice to cap the elevation. However this is very far removed from pastiche – the contrasting pre-patinated copper cladding to the entire building is highly distinctive, and merges well with the predominantly stone finish of the buildings of the street.

Convention has been denied in carrying the same high quality materials and design round into the narrow Mitchell Lane. Among the few concessions to stylistic traits current at the time is the treatment of the window openings which are splayed at the corners, with the feature carried into the bands above and below the window apertures, providing a repetitive decorative pattern. The windows to the upper storeys are consummately proportioned.

In providing this highly contextual response to the streetscape, the architects have eschewed the opportunity to increase the number of storeys and the height of the building, thereby lifting the scale of the city, from which so many modern developments suffer. It is fully deserving of the historian Charles McKean's claim that it remains "probably Glasgow's most subtle post-war infill building".

BOAC Building

Royal Commonwealth Pool

Dalkeith Road, Edinburgh

Robert Matthew, Johnson-Marshall & Partners

WHILE THE BRIEF FOR the pool, built for the 1970 Commonwealth Games, was not altogether dissimilar to that for the Dollan Aqua Centre, the sensitivity of the corner site on Dalkeith Road, with its backdrop of Salisbury Crags, demanded a more restrained architectural response.

Architect John Richards, blessed with the virtue of being self-effacing, sought later to justify the quality of the design of the building as having flowed solely from the requirements of the brief. While that is not in dispute he was also referring obliquely to the transition that had occurred within the practice.

Robert Matthew's aim in the 1950s had been to embrace the International Modern Movement, but this had resulted in a playful, more romantic style of modernism. Richards, in referring to his own architectural training, recalled the exhortation to avoid sentimentality, and his professed admiration for the work

Royal Commonwealth Pool
© Grant Bulloch

of Richard Neutra finds expression here in the long, overlapping planes of the elevations floating above a plinth of blue engineering brick.

On the principal elevation to Dalkeith Road the uninterrupted floor and roof plates, clad in white precast concrete and aluminium respectively, are satisfyingly counterpoised with the tall flue. The very large footprint and bulk of the building are disguised by the intelligent disposition of the elements of the brief, using the slope on the site to considerable advantage.

Once entered, the building has an unexpectedly complex spatial quality. The clean lines of the poolside areas, designed to house 1,700 spectators, are achieved only through having adopted an integrated approach to architecture and engineering, by which the challenges of a highly serviced building type such as this were resolved.

Bernat Klein Design Studio

Galashiels, Scottish Borders

Peter Womersley

FIFTEEN YEARS HAD ELAPSED from when Peter Womersley completed High Sunderland for the celebrated textile designer Bernat Klein, when the design studio was delivered to the same client. The inspiration for both designs had their origins in the transatlantic houses of the International Modern Movement, but in designing the studio, the architect was responding to a fundamentally different brief. The principal studio space was to be divided into four zones consisting of a service core, a studio for painting, a meeting space and textile showroom, and an area for relaxation and informal discussion.

Positioned with considerable care within a mature woodland setting, the main studio floor was placed at first floor, with the stair tower continuing upwards to a roof terrace. The bridge had not been planned originally. It had to be introduced to meet fire regulations, but it allows the studio to be approached and experienced in an entirely unforgettable way with the breathtaking views over the stunning rolling Borders landscape unfurling with every step.

The open plan layout centred around the service core with the floor plates cantilevered from slender columns, recalling the German master, Mies van der Rohe's plan for the Farnsworth House, although Womersley acknowledged a debt to Frank Lloyd Wright's 'Fallingwater'.

Whereas the earlier house was essentially of lightweight construction, the studio celebrates the confident use of modern construction and materials unusual for a structure of this domestic scale – reinforced concrete troughs for the floor plates, blue engineering brick, steel, and corners of mitred glass so as not to impede the views. The cantilevered floor plates defy the heaviness of their construction, appearing to hover within the landscape.

Phase III Housing

Woodside Development Area 'A', St George's Road, Glasgow

Boswell, Mitchell and Johnston

WOODSIDE WAS THE LAST of the Comprehensive Development Areas to be designated to solve Glasgow's acute post-war housing problems. Shoehorning the development onto a narrow site of three acres alongside the busy St George's Road, the architects worked closely with the housing managers in creating a balanced social mix of 215 dwellings, of which 32 units were four-apartment family houses.

Two eight-storey slab blocks were designed, linked by a five-storey block incorporating communal areas for drying and services. The section through the blocks was ingenious, and by adopting maisonettes with internal stairs, the need for external deck access was reduced. Externally, the blocks are uncompromising, with the stairs and lifts at the outer extremities of the blocks set within separate towers with flying bridge links to the access decks.

The architecture is assured – the south-facing elevations are heavily modelled to break down the scale of the blocks through introducing angled window bays, creating visual interest in the shadows cast from the bold pattern-making of verticals and horizontals. Inspiration was found from the traditional form of the Glasgow tenement, while the colour of the brickwork recalls the red sandstone used across the city.

The brickwork is beautifully detailed throughout, giving the blocks a monolithic appearance and, significantly, it has been well-maintained. On St George's Road the access deck is lifted marginally above the level of the pavement to give privacy, and small gardens are introduced where the apartments face south. There are parallels here with the pioneering social housing schemes by Darbourne & Darke at Pimlico and Islington, and in embracing the contemporary theories of "defensible space" promoted by Jane Jacobs and Oscar Newman.

Phase III Housing
© Andrew Wright

137

University of Stirling

Airthrey Road, Bridge of Allan

Robert Matthew, Johnson-Marshall & Partners

THE 1963 ROBBINS REPORT resulted in the establishment of seven new universities across the UK, all of them to be housed in parkland settings. Stirling University was the only new campus in Scotland, for which the chosen site was the exceptional 300-acre late eighteenth century designed landscape of Robert Adam's Airthrey Castle.

The success of the masterplan lay in the integration of the new teaching, residential and administration buildings with the landscape and woodland. With the exception of the Pathfoot Building, the focus is always on the artificial loch. As the first building to be completed, the Pathfoot preceded the Royal Commonwealth Pool, but the design ethos is essentially the same shared direct architectural language of long horizontal planes, of precast concrete with a distinctive white aggregate, contrasting with the topography of the site. With spur corridors and glazed internal courtyards, the layout is imbued with a Scandinavian character, reminiscent of Arne Jacobsen's much admired Munkegard School in Copenhagen.

A steel-framed structure, it was erected at breakneck speed, allowing for complete flexibility as the early needs of the institution changed, and expanded.

The Pathfoot set the highest standards for the buildings on the campus that followed within the space of a few years. Floating above the loch, and leading to the student residences, a footbridge is sparsely elegant.

Between the spurs of the residential blocks stepping up the slope, lawns are laid out where the sun can be soaked up and the views enjoyed. The architects had been engaged also by the University of York, but John Richards' design for Stirling marks an altogether more convincing and mature response to the opportunities of a glorious setting.

University of Stirling

ABOVE
© RCAHMS. Licensor www.scran.ac.uk

FAR LEFT
© Jean O'Reilly

LEFT
© Grant Bulloch

Ranald MacInnes

RANALD MACINNES IS Head of Special Projects at the newly-established public body Historic Environment Scotland which was formed as a merger of the Royal Commission on the Ancient and Historical Monuments of Scotland and Historic Scotland. He began his career with English Heritage in the 1980s and has a special interest in 20th-century architecture and planning.

Ranald is an Honorary Research Fellow of the Institute of Art History, University of Glasgow, Visiting Lecturer in Architectural Design for the Conservation of Built Heritage at the University of Strathclyde and a former chair of Docomomo Scotland. He has published books, essays, articles and reviews on architectural history and conservation.

1976-1985

ESSAYS BY RANALD MacINNES

Eden Court Theatre
© Keith Hunter

Eden Court Theatre

Bishop's Road, Inverness
Law and Dunbar-Nasmith

BUILT AS A CIVIC CENTRE for performing arts, the theatre was designed to accommodate concerts, opera, ballet, drama, conferences, dances and film. An important public commission, the complex represents an early attempt to design boldly but sympathetically within an historic setting.

This stunning building is linked to the town's nineteenth century Bishop's Palace, creatively converted as a 'servant' building to house dressing rooms, a green room and office space. The complex was an interface of old and new, expressed in a geometric cluster often seen in late-modern compositions where there was a

desire to 'break up' the strong outlines of earlier Brutalist or modernist setpieces.

Hexagonal glazed projections with individual, slated pitched roofs pay homage to the historic context and mask the large, simple forms to the rear. Internally, the suspended foyer and staircases are encased within hexagonal glass walls creating novel, outward-looking spaces with dramatic landscape views. Traditionally, theatres had sought to create an enclosed, internal and atmospheric world but the Eden Court complex, especially because of its wider, civic and conference roles, connects with its context, and challenges – in a

modernist manner – the inside/outside barrier.

Anticipating later architectural moves, the foyer is a kind of paved 'street' incorporating ticket office and cloakrooms on the blind inner face and a restaurant and bar within the externally-expressed hexagons. The 800-seater auditorium with its thrust stage is on a traditional horseshoe plan with cantilevered circle and upper circle. With its sparkling, crystalline forms, the Eden Court is, almost literally, the jewel in the crown of Inverness's heritage. In 2004-7, the complex was extended to provide an additional theatre space, cinemas, and studios.

Scottish Amicable Life Assurance Society Headquarters

St Vincent Street, Glasgow

King, Main & Ellison

THE PRACTICE OF King, Main & Ellison designed several high quality commercial buildings in central Glasgow in the years 1965-88 where they responded to changing architectural demands within a modernist constructional framework of steelwork and curtain walling. The bright and bold pastel colours of Fitzpatrick House, Wellington Street (1965, demolished 1989) had demanded attention in a crowded commercial architectural environment. However by the mid-1970s the subtly contextual massing of the Scottish Amicable Life Assurance Society building instead played down its size and presence – its apparent bulk – on one of Glasgow's most prestigious commercial streets.

The materials used speak of the blue chip, corporate modernism of the sixties and seventies: gold-tinted glass, polished granite, an expression of expensive solidity and durability. The technically and technologically confident, sleek and beautifully engineered composition masks the scale of a very large and potentially overpowering building by projecting, receding, rising and falling and by responding to the significant change in ground level with the introduction of a courtyard garden.

The composition is made up of bays whose size is approximately that of eighteenth century Glasgow house plots which we see extended dramatically upwards next door at James Salmon Junior's 'Hatrack' of 1899, which the Scottish Amicable references in its soaring glass 'towers'. While the exterior is expressed in an episodic way to break down its external impact, paradoxically perhaps, the building was constructed on a six-metre structural grid to maximise the endless internal flexibility that successful business needed and an uninterrupted floorplate can offer.

The Scottish Amicable Building is well worthy of its St Vincent Street setting among some of Glasgow's most dynamic historic commercial and ecclesiastical buildings.

Scottish Amicable Life Assurance Society Headquarters

1979

Church of St John Ogilvie

Bourtreehill, Irvine

Clunie Rowell with Douglas Niven and Gerry Connolly

BY THE LATE 1970S, when St John Ogilvie Church was built on the edge of Irvine New Town, the post-war church-building boom was all but over. In line with, and, perhaps even ahead, of other building types, churches had witnessed an unprecedented bout of confident experimentation in planning and design which left a legacy in Scotland of remarkably radical and often uplifting architecture.

Internationally, churches had been seeking to redefine their architectural and social presence within communities and Scotland was no different. Lacking an 'establishment' formula in any of the denominations, a free and open attitude to new church design had produced an amazing range of architectural solutions.

Typically, the new Church of St John Ogilvie was boldly conceived and very much a landscape 'event' designed to play an architectural part in defining place and community. Gillespie, Kidd and Coia's earlier ecclesiastical work had demonstrated the flexibility of form possible in Catholic worship, and the further response at St John Ogilvie was to compress a very Scottish ecclesiastical complex of church, hall and presbytery into a single composition, responding, in fact, more to Presbyterian than to Catholic prototypes.

Many earlier modernist churches had toyed with skeletal or token spires but St John Ogilvie dispenses with the feature altogether while alluding to it by means of a striking octagonal pyramid roof. The notional 'spire' is thereby placed at the centre of the plan and the form becomes almost pre-Christian in its simplicity. Internally, the use of directed light on and through everyday building materials, together with the artfully pegged roof structure, recalls Charles Rennie Mackintosh's take on Arts and Crafts, and underscores the simple 'worshipful' ambience of the space.

Cummins Engine Factory Extension

Shottskirk Road, Shotts

Ahrends, Burton & Koralek

THE HEAD OF CUMMINS Diesel Engines of Columbus, Indiana had been a long-standing patron of cutting-edge architecture (including his house designed by Eero Saarinen) when he commissioned a new factory from one of the UK's leading modernist practices. An earlier Cummins plant at Darlington by Kevin Roche, John Dinkeloo Associates (1966) had brought great architectural refinement to factory architecture but this was not followed up significantly, and anxieties about 'big sheds' persisted.

The Cummins factory at Shotts was, in theory, no more than a linked procession of big sheds. The answer to the monotony that such a process risked creating was provided through a brilliant amalgam of self-conscious modernist references, along with up-to-date pace-setting. This included: space-age forms; soaring tent-like structures (seemingly tethered rather than planted); a functionalist composition recalling the iconic van Nelle factory and its pioneering Dutch contemporaries; 'high-tech' exposed and colour-coded services, revisiting the hugely popular Pompidou Centre in Paris; and a setting of striking pyramidal grassed earthworks by James Hope, inspired by the industrial spoil heaps of central Scotland.

Inside, the factory was clean, humane, and planned well to suit the business of producing diesel engines but also of taking care of the highly-skilled workforce who had been extensively consulted as part of the design process. All of this served to remind people that architecture could bring joy to industry *itself* and not just to the showy offices fronting the works of big industrial complexes.

A little over a year later, the same firm of architects was chosen to design the Hampton wing of the National Gallery in London, sadly subsequently cancelled, a great opportunity lost.

Pitlochry Festival Theatre

Port-na-craig Road, Pitlochry

Law and Dunbar-Nasmith

PITLOCHRY FESTIVAL THEATRE was founded by John Stewart in 1951 and famously began life in a marquee. The choice of Law and Dunbar-Nasmith to design a permanent venue recognised their experience of theatre projects. Community-orientated theatre had enjoyed something of a heyday in the sixties and seventies at Cumbernauld, the Byre (St Andrews) and other locations where the 'rep' tradition was channelled in new cultural directions, and community theatres began to embrace music, dance and wider community and public uses.

The obvious exemplar for Pitlochry was the beautiful, scenographic design by the same firm at the recently completed Eden Court Theatre, Inverness that was as much a civic complex as a traditional theatre. The Pitlochry design, which is carefully crafted into its landscape setting, is recessive and unassuming, constructed from brown brick on the entrance façade that fades into its landscape surroundings. However, it is a building with two faces.

Inside, a cantilevered glazed foyer overlooks the banks of the River Tummel and the town of Pitlochry. Seen from the town, the glazed symmetry of the original composition has something of the elegance and composure if not the materiality of the Scottish country house about it, a fitting exemplar for a building in the landscape. It is an undoubtedly beautiful, unexpectedly light and airy theatre complex that responds to its pure Highland setting.

The firm has maintained its specialisation in the restoration and extension of historic theatres, and in the creation of new ones. Pitlochry Festival Theatre was itself upgraded and extended by the practice in 1998 in the form of a low glass wing to provide a restaurant and improved front-of-house facilities.

Dundee Repertory Theatre

Tay Square, Dundee

Nicoll Russell Studios

THE THEATRE WAS BUILT as a permanent home for the Dundee 'Rep' with public funds and donations that outstripped all expectations. The public enthusiasm for live theatre in Scotland as a prerequisite of urban living is quite remarkable. Although a 'contextual' building – that is designed with its historic setting in Tay Square in mind – the theatre is rarely photographed in context. Indeed, this is true of many good buildings with similar aspirations. In celebrating their achievement in respecting and enhancing their urban context, perversely we see them standing alone.

Nicoll Russell Studio's award-winning response to the brief was 'modern monumental', a device for expressing the civic importance of the building within the scope of a very tight budget. Great, shaped blocks are set up in an informal post and lintel arrangement in step with the postmodern journey towards

classicism by way of apparently plainly expressed structure.

The front-of-house interior is fully expressed on the exterior, lightly glazed so that the concrete staircase seems caught between the two conditions, invitingly open and accessible in the way that later twentieth century theatres wished so much to be. Lit up at night, the effect of openness is even more pronounced.

As with many buildings of the period, in a modernist renewal of the Arts and Crafts vow, a virtue is made of the rough texture of inexpensive materials. In the wrong hands, a move like this has a dispiriting effect but expertly done, as at Dundee Rep, it imbues texture and interest. Nicoll Russell Studios went on to design the new Byre Theatre for St Andrews in 2002.

The Burrell Collection

Pollok Park, Glasgow

Barry Gasson, Brit Andreson and John Meunier

THE BURRELL COLLECTION IS an outstanding, bespoke museum of international importance. Like most great modern buildings, it is a significant example of existing or developing tendencies in later twentieth century architecture: the primacy of user experience over architectural effect; the power of place and landscape; the concept of 'megastructure' where many functions are layered into one complex composition; and an immateriality denying the wall and encouraging buildings to float between interior and exterior. The parkland setting of the Burrell is a key part of the architectural concept, with the workaday elements of the museum out of sight below the galleries to preserve the purity of the visitor experience.

The project was won in architectural competition in 1971. Paradoxically, the design stood out because of its non-rhetorical, low-lying integration with the landscape, a design feature that suggests Scandinavian precedents, a victory of craft and materiality over style. The design was also a cultural bridgehead – an early example of an 'iconic' building that would spearhead Glasgow's amazing cultural revival during the 1980s and beyond.

The gallery provides an inspiring setting for shipping magnate Sir William Burrell's vast collection of art and antiquities, bequeathed to Glasgow in 1944 under strict conditions that the collection would be kept unified and housed well away from the city's industrial pollution. Burrell's dining room with its contents and those of other rooms was to be reconstructed within the new gallery. The enormous and varied collection consists of over 8.000 items and many important architectural fragments have been incorporated into the building. The aim of the designers was to allow the objects to 'speak' and the gallery to be silent.

The Burrell Collection
TOP AND OPPOSITE PAGE
© Keith Hunter
ABOVE
© Ruairidh Moir

155

Ingram Square
ABOVE
© Jean O'Reilly
RIGHT
© Jon Jardine

Ingram Square

Ingram Street, Candleriggs, Brunswick Street and Wilson Street, Glasgow

Elder and Cannon Architects

IF ELDER AND CANNON'S WORK were limited only to their interventions over time at Ingram Square we would still have a significant achievement which lays out the firm's – and the city's – architectural evolution over twenty years. The modern Merchant City is Glasgow's great contribution to urban renewal. It is a powerful contribution that begins with the pioneering conservation developers Kantel tapping into and powerfully developing a regeneration effort aimed at retaining and growing the inner city's population, and creating a lively new urban centre for culture and entertainment.

The scheme at the heart of the project was an entire city block called Ingram Square. The square is inverted, with its 'inhabited wall' to the street and two inner courtyards – a carefully articulated 'block within a block'. Most of the surviving historic warehouses (including Robert Billings' 1854 Houndsditch Building) were converted to flats with some shops, but selected buildings in the block were taken down and replaced with architecture that is clearly postmodern in inspiration but with none of the superficiality and applied detailing associated with the earlier versions of that style.

Elder and Cannon's celebrated corner block on Wilson Street remains a model of intervention in an historic setting: bold and gutsy with a scale and proportion of openings related to both materials and context. Like most good buildings it seemed like a piece of instant heritage. Kantel's scheme also allowed for the story to continue within an urban framework that was flexible yet fixed enough to become, over time, an architectural narrative about Glasgow's urban renaissance, and about a particular architects practice's commitment and contribution to that project.

Caley House

Howgate, Kilwinning

Irvine Development Corporation

OVER THE PERIOD OF THE life of Irvine Development Corporation, whose remit extended to the nearby town of Kilwinning, a wide variety of housing to suit all needs was developed. The Corporation employed several of Scotland's most talented architects. Their work can be seen throughout the new town.

The cutting edge modernism of earlier housing – boldly set against the heritage of the surviving historic burgh architecture – gave way in the 1980s to an increasingly contextual, conservation-orientated infill. The story of Scotland's architecture from the 1960s to the 90s could be told in this one location, where

bright, younger architects were given the freedom to express contemporary ideas.

The much admired, multi-award winning Caley House was designed by Roan Rutherford of the Corporation for the YMCA/YWCA. The building provides housing and communal facilities for sixty young single people in accommodation ranging from one to four person flats set out under a unifying, wide slate roof incorporating engaged 'conservatory' spaces.

The complex responds to a vernacular context of materials, form and street pattern, yet is framed still within an essentially modernist community-needs concept. The gridded fenestration picks

up, perhaps, on a postmodern Scottish renewed or revived interest in Charles Rennie Mackintosh, seen first at Gillespie, Kidd and Coia's Robinson College, Cambridge (1977) and later referenced in many prestigious Scottish commissions, such as the National Library of Scotland's Map Annexe at Causewayside, Edinburgh (1987) by Andrew Merrylees.

The swansong of Irvine Development Corporation's architecture came with the 1996 development of Irvine Harbour, again by Roan Rutherford. There he created a tidy streetscape of more overtly historicist tenements as a backdrop to the existing heritage setting.

Caley House
© Christopher Marr

Babbity Bowster
ABOVE
© Jon Jardine
OPPOSITE PAGE
© Jean O'Reilly

Babbity Bowster

Blackfriars Street, Glasgow

Nicholas Groves-Raines Architects

THE WONDERFUL BOUTIQUE hotel and restaurant, 'Babbity Bowster' takes its name from an old Scottish country dance. An eighteenth century building, a run-down relic of a half-completed urban design scheme by the Adam brothers, was rescued by one of a new breed of urban conservationists for the restaurateur Fraser Laurie by Nicholas Groves-Raines Architects working with Tom Laurie Associates. The architect sought preservation by intervention – in this case, the entire top floor and pediment of the building were reinstated.

The intervention had its roots in the can-do 'conservation by occupation'

schemes of Fraser's brother Tom, who had helped rescue the Tron Kirk on Chisholm Street – another Adam survivor of sorts – as a city theatre. It was the kind of direct action to preserve heritage in the days before it became a 'sector'. The nearby Café Gandolfi, complete with Tim Stead furniture and stained glass by John K Clark (opened as long ago as 1979), had led the way in the creation of the Merchant City's new profile as a place to eat, drink and be arty.

It is hard to believe that the city's empty and foreboding Georgian streets with their nineteenth and twentieth century warehouses were so swiftly

and dramatically transformed by one of the UK's earliest and most successful regeneration schemes. The repair and re-modelling of Babbity Bowster and its new/old conversion helped set the seal on Glasgow's amazing urban chic. Highly improbable as it seemed as late as 1980, heritage was now edgy and contemporary. The food, the ambience, the enchanting painted decoration, the cosy fire and the impromptu folk music of Babbity Bowster is pure Glasgow magic.

Sarah Pearce

SARAH STUDIED ARCHITECTURAL History at the University of Edinburgh before graduating MA in 2012. She then spent two years with the Scottish Historic Buildings Trust where she assisted with preparation for the Riddle's Court restoration project and the management of the Trust's rescued buildings.

In 2014, Sarah moved to the Architectural Heritage Society of Scotland (AHSS) as their Development Officer. Since then, a key focus has been on the campaign to find an appropriate use for the former Royal High School in Edinburgh, bringing the Society in to the digital age and promoting its work within the sector. Sarah volunteers on the AHSS Forth & Borders Cases Panel (amongst other social activities) and is an Affiliate Member of the Institute of Historic Building Conservation.

1986-1995

ESSAYS BY SARAH PEARCE

Grianan Building

Dundee Technology Park, Dundee

Nicoll Russell Studios

DOUBTLESS SEEKING TO AVOID the often temporary and soulless feel of business parks and office buildings; Nicoll Russell Studios looked to the original cottage that stood on the site of the new Dundee Technology Park to draw inspiration for their 'landmark' building. The Grianan Building was to be the first structure on the site of what was then a new park and was a speculative office construction. It aimed to inspire the aesthetic trend of the whole site to be more imaginative and to encourage businesses to take up residence.

It was originally hoped that the original Grianan (Gaelic for 'sunny place') cottage could be incorporated into the final structure. However it became apparent in the design process that this was just not feasible. Instead, inspiration was taken from the stonework and the interaction between inside and outside spaces. The design in essence, is four squares within a square. One square is utilised as a walled, courtyard car park, whilst the remaining three are the office spaces. The squares are connected through a two storey, glass, reception lobby.

Set within its own parkland environment, this elegant stone and glass pavilion greets visitors on arrival but only reveals the interest of the masonry courtyard walls once the main entrance has been reached. A relatively limited palette of high quality materials are articulated here with great success. Windows are formed from inwardly sloping glass, connected to upwardly sloping ceilings, thus providing glare-free daylight to the internal work spaces. These innovative forms and ideas are what we might expect from the architects who sparked the initial design for the brilliant, Falkirk Wheel.

Grianan Building

Princes Square
© Jean O'Reilly

Princes Square

Buchanan Street, Glasgow

Hugh Martin & Partners

THIS RENOVATION PROJECT incorporates a wide range of artistic and craft skills. Princes Square is not just another shopping centre. Hugh Martin and Partners had worked primarily on large commercial and office projects (such as the – love it or loathe it – St James Centre in Edinburgh) between their founding in 1969 and 2009, when they joined the SMC Group.

In 1986 their project to revamp the historic Princes Square and form a shopping centre from an open courtyard was a challenging one. The result is something really special. The architects decided to cover the cobbled square with a vast, vaulted, glass dome and insert new internal walkways and socialising spaces. The combination of the symmetrical criss-cross escalators, spiral staircases and towering vertical white pillars creates a most enjoyable experience.

The glass roof allows daylight to penetrate the vast internal atrium, suggesting that, though the shopper is not quite outside, nor are they entirely indoors either. The historic charm of the 1840s square remains through the retention of the original frontages with their polished sandstone façades and canopied entrances.

The giant metal peacock that acts as a figurehead to the main entrance is a striking contrast to the restrained and elegant building that it sits atop. Indeed, it begins the exciting and unexpected Art Nouveau theme that continues internally. The sculptural metalwork that forms the balustrading of the public walkways speaks to the botanically styled lampposts, all created by Alan Dawson. The trompe l'oeil wall paintings of famous Glaswegians which once adorned the central escalator, were created by Dai Vaughan. Despite their sad demise, this award-winning creation is still great fun.

National Library of Scotland Map Annexe

Causewayside, Edinburgh

Andrew Merrylees Associates

ANDREW MERRYLEES, A FORMER partner at Sir Basil Spence, Glover & Ferguson, reportedly designed the entire Causewayside library building around the module of the bookshelves to be housed there, 900mm. This dictated the floor panels, window panes and internal partitions. This stylish design has an entirely functional purpose; routing as many services as possible around the exterior of the building, to leave the interior to focus on its task – chiefly, housing and storing Scotland's map collection, of around two million items.

At each storey, the floor plates are constructed for great load-bearing capacity, prepared for the National Library's ever growing collection. The glazing is orientated to the north and UV filtered to avoid any chance of damage to the precious contents. The height of the building speaks to its neighbours on the east and the west. The former is lower in

scale, the latter is bolder. Even so, the full 19,000m² size of the building is hidden, it continues a further two and a half storeys below ground.

The design is bold and unapologetic. The square glazing and steel structure with stone from Newbigging Quarry (specially re-opened for this project) make quite the impact on this main approach from the south. It appears as if building blocks have been playfully assembled, with the bright yellow staircases visible from the outside.

There are hints of Mackintosh's geometric Art Nouveau here, melded with traditional Scottish forms into an altogether contemporary composition. Twelve Scottish artists were commissioned to create panels to be laminated within the window glazing for added decoration. A £10 million redevelopment programme is due to complete in 2017.

National Library of Scotland Annexe
© Keith Hunter

169

General Accident Fire and Life Assurance Corporation Headquarters
© Keith Hunter

General Accident Fire and Life Assurance Corporation Headquarters

Necessity Brae, Perth

James Parr & Partners

FOUNDED IN PERTH IN 1885, the General Accident Fire and Life Assurance Corporation grew to become one of the largest insurance companies in the UK. By the late 1970s the decision was taken to commission a very substantial new national headquarters on the hilly site of the 18-acre, Pitheavlis Farm, just outside Perth.

The enticing ziggurat design of stepped layers, emerging from the hillside, certainly makes an impression. The vast structure houses not only offices but also an integrated sports complex and a staff hostel. Delicate internal details include rosewood panelling in the boardroom, a tapestry in the foyer by artist Sam Ainsley, batik panels by Norma Starszakowna and a ceramic wall, featuring the names of select employees, by Mike de Hann. The integration of this range of impressive artwork into such a boldly contemporary building attracted a Saltire Award.

From its founding in 1956, James Parr and Partners had grown to become one of the largest UK architects practices of the era. They had worked on a great range of projects before this £30m commission, from supermarkets to private houses, banks to churches, including work for General Accident as early as 1963 when the practice had undertaken extensive alteration work to the insurance company's previous headquarters in Perth.

The lengthy gestation of this new, out-of-town, headquarters complex is testament, not merely to its scale and complexity, but to the level of exacting care and deliberation over this bold concrete and glass edifice and the commissioning of the range of artwork both internal and external, which adorns it. This truly exciting design in a very visible location not only takes on the topography of the site but enhances it.

Carrick Quay

Clyde Street, Glasgow

Davis Duncan Partnership

ONE OF THE FIRST MAJOR projects to regenerate the banks of the Clyde, following its loss of industry; Carrick Quay was one of the most significant inner-city speculative developments in the UK in the late 1980s. Taking inspiration from its namesake, the world's oldest surviving clipper ship (the, Sunderland built, *City of Adelaide*, 1864, subsequently HMS *Carrick* then *The Carrick* and now berthed in Adelaide under her original name), which floated in the water just opposite for a number of years, the design is thoroughly nautical in theme.

The area around the former Glasgow Fishmarket (now regenerated as the Briggait Artists' Studios) was very run down. This development was an important forerunner to major riverside redevelopment. The design resulted from a (very) limited competition. Four firms submitted ideas with Davis Duncan's scheme very much preferred.

Carrick Quay

From the entrance 'gangplanks' leading from the street to the lobby areas, to the guardrailed balconies with timber decking attached to each south facing flat, the maritime references are to the fore. The building is crowned with a continuous balcony running along the façade at penthouse level, almost like the upper deck of a ship. Above this, project a number of 'crows nests' offering the ultimate view of the Clyde and the landscape beyond.

Following its success in the competition to win the project, the aim of the very innovative residential developer, The Burrell Company, working with the Davis Duncan Partnership, was to create an iconic 'ocean liner' of 93 flats and penthouses of top quality riverfront accommodation. This was certainly achieved and was undoubtedly the catalyst to significant further regeneration in the area.

The Italian Centre

John Street, Glasgow

Page\Park Architects

THE ITALIAN CENTRE WAS AN early success for Page\Park Architects. A mix of old and new, with a strong artistic element and Italian flair, this mixed use residential/retail/office development has become one of the most popular developments of its type in Glasgow.

By the 1980s the Merchant City area had become very run down and was littered with publicly owned buildings with little or often no use. Page\Park's client, Classical House Ltd, took the bold move of selective demolition of warehouse buildings and the retention of key, tenemental stone façades. This allowed the creation of an internal courtyard and a fronting little 'piazza', on John Street, both beautifully executed.

The development embraced an exciting mix of modern sculpture in its central courtyard space with Shona Kinloch's joyous man and dog sculptures looking upwards and edgy steelwork friezes and jaggy figurative sculpture by Jack Sloan attached to the new buildings. By way of contrast, the sculptures by Alexander Stoddart at roof level and the 'Mercury' within the piazza respect the restraint of the development's historic exterior. These architectural and sculptural juxtapositions emphasised the importance of valuing the original fabric of the nineteenth century buildings, retaining Glasgow's strong historic identity, yet allowing room for change and innovative design.

The new-build elements are contextual in scale and proportion, yet contemporary in their detailing. This Italian piazza environment, complete with covered walkways, outside dining, nude bronze classical messenger and rooftop 'Italia' was an early precedent for Glasgow's new 'urban village' lifestyle – a place to live, shop, work, eat and have fun – very Notting Hill!

Fruitmarket Gallery
© Grant Bulloch

Fruitmarket Gallery

Market Street, Edinburgh

Richard Murphy Architects

A **TURNING POINT FOR** architecture in Edinburgh, Richard Murphy and then business partner, Graeme Montgomery's upgrade of the Fruitmarket Gallery showed how historic buildings could be handled in a modern way, without resorting to pastiche. Built around 1931, the former fruit and vegetable market, had evolved to become a gallery, a key location for the contemporary art scene in the city in 1974. By the late 1980s a facelift was long overdue. However once the design process began it was clear that a little more intervention was needed.

The original stone façade on Market Street was uninviting, barely communicating to passers-by that this was a public building. This was improved by the complete removal of one section of the elevation, at both ground and first floor levels, allowing both improved access and daylight penetration. On the upper floor a hoist was located in the new opening, thus allowing large scale artworks to be manoeuvred with relative ease. Further sections of the façade were replaced with large glass panels, creating a more transparent face, where visitors can instantly see the bookshop, café and through to the exhibition spaces.

Internally a very simple layout centres upon an industrial steel staircase that can be lifted to facilitate large installations. The most striking improvement however, was the floating winged roof. An aluminium construction with integrated rooflights, lightly resting on a further insertion of clerestory windows, soars over the external walls. This simultaneously brings more natural light in to the building, adds much needed height to the top floor and opens it up to views of the city's most celebrated landmarks.

Challenge House

Canal Street, Glasgow

McNeish Design Partnership

THIS INNOVATIVE WEDGE PLAN design is a positive response to its unusual plot, located directly adjacent to the M8 motorway from which it is an arresting sight. The triangular form sees the hypotenuse run parallel to the main road, the shortest side of the building run up against its second boundary and leaves room for highly desirable car parking to the front.

One of the most striking aspects of the building is how comfortably it fulfils its mixed use function. It not only houses office space and two apartments, but also warehousing and meeting rooms for 12 different organisations, over quite a compact four storeys. Aluminium 'rainscreen' cladding is used to great effect on this project (among the first uses of this technology in Scotland), emphasising the modernist design of clean lines and sharp finishes. Open-grate maintenance walkways cast decorative shadows on bright days.

What perhaps makes this structure stand out from the crowd, is that the lead architect, Grant Robertson, chose to address the location as opposed to trying to ignore it. This was achieved through the extensive use of windows on all three façades, unashamedly declaring its presence, whilst generating a light and airy interior. Extensive double glazing dealt with noise pollution.

Intentionally low tech, the building was low budget, with the internal fitting-out by the client, the Christian Resource Centre. Its high visibility is a declaration of positive intent. It has also been acknowledged that the reason this design succeeded so well, was due to the free hand given by the project patron and generous benefactor, Jim McLellan of Peebles, without whom it could not have been realised.

Challenge House

178-180 Ingram Street
RIGHT
© Jon Jardine
OPPOSITE PAGE
© Jean O'Reilly

178-180 Ingram Street

Glasgow

Page\Park Architects

THIS BUILDING REPLACES A commercial block destroyed by fire in 1992. It takes its proportions from the original and is clad in stone, but is otherwise crisp and contemporary, its exterior raised well above the ordinary by its sculptural detailing. There are spiky heavily patinated phosphor-bronze shutters to second floor façade windows, attractive bronze surrounds to the first floor windows and a unique group of sculptured heads. This cranked up level of decoration is warranted in the context of the stripped down modernism of the building itself and the simple traditional aesthetic of the buildings on either side, including the only slightly older Italian Centre

There is a glass canopy over the ground floor walkway giving shelter to visitors. While this detail and the shutters are contemporary, the rest of the applied detailing is in a more classical idiom. Atop the ground floor pilasters, small bronze portrait castings by Alexander Stoddart, depict men who helped to shape the Merchant City: the builder and mason Mungo Naismith (1730-1770), architect David Hamilton (1768-1843), plasterer Thomas Clayton (1710-1760) and merchant builder Allan Dreghorn (1706-1764). Stoddart's sculpture is ideally suited to public monuments and to the integrated enrichment of an architecture rooted in classical tradition. His repose and restraint contrasts with the aggressively stylised shutters by Jack Sloan.

This building harmonises well with the Italian Centre where there is more levity in the artworks. This is particularly evident in the internal courtyard with its rill and Shona Kinloch's whimsical sculpture. In fact, to encourage Italian-themed retail and restaurants, the marketing slogan coined by the developers was the inspired, 'Put Some Dolce Into Your Vita'.

A. JACOBSON & CO. LTD.

Brunswick Hotel
© Keith Hunter

Brunswick Hotel

Brunswick Street, Glasgow
Elder and Cannon Architects

BRIDGING THE GAP BETWEEN the French Renaissance and the 'bizarre gothic' of its neighbours in the centre of Glasgow's Merchant City, stands the Brunswick Hotel. Completed in 1995, this building was an infill addition to Ingram Square. It filled the last gap in a large city block where an innovative mix of new-build and warehouse reconfiguration had been carefully nurtured by Elder and Cannon since the early 1980s.

A difficult gap site to design for, the hotel cleverly bonds the disjointed street roofline from south to north with a giant 'Z' step in stone. This in turn is over-arched by a curved copper-clad timber roof, creating a striking double-height rooftop apartment within. Exposed steel supports at the edges of the building add a transparency to the eight-storey, three-bay structure.

This subtle, yet intriguing building is a welcome addition to the Merchant City conservation area and has a pleasing integrity in an area where many developers have opted for façade retention. The largely pedestrianised street is particularly well suited to the glass fronted, ground floor restaurant that, in clement weather, spills out, pleasantly onto the street. The design, pragmatically, has the protection required for the local climate. A suspended glass canopy is set above the immediate external area.

Identifying itself as the "only small independent contemporary hotel in Glasgow City Centre" this purpose built hotel was clearly designed with function at the very forefront and has served this niche purpose well. With clever compact spaces internally (styled by Graven Images), there is a great sense of welcome and character.

Ruairidh Moir RIAS

RUAIRIDH MOIR HAILS FROM Tolsta on the Isle of Lewis and trained at the University of Strathclyde School of Architecture where he now teaches in the 2nd year design studio. He also gained an international perspective whilst studying in Barcelona, later returning to work at Miralles Tagliabue EMBT.

Since graduation, Ruairidh has worked on a variety of projects through a new venture named BARD which aims to realise projects produced with an emphasis on artisan craft and a focus on experiment. In 2015 he was elected onto RIAS council. He enjoys writing on architecture and playing a proactive role in the profession. Ruairidh is particularly interested in culture, history and theory in architecture and art.

1996-2005

ESSAYS BY RUAIRIDH MOIR RIAS

National Museum of Scotland

Bristo Place, Edinburgh

Benson + Forsyth

IN THE 1980S THE National Museum proposed an extension to house its dedicated Scottish collection resulting in the selection of Benson + Forsyth by competition in 1991. Their proposal, realised, not without controversy, over eight years, has produced a highly individual building with an arresting presence. The role of the competition chairman, the late Sixth Marquess of Bute, in delivering this powerful masterpiece cannot be underestimated.

Adjoining Captain Fowke's original building, the extension has respected its site and context by its mass and material selection. An ensemble of simple forms confidently arranged, its surfaces have been carved into, pitted and excavated, much like the artefacts contained within. Chosen for its significance and august appearance, the blonde sandstone is this building's principal protagonist and clads the distinctive corner drum and adjoining façades. This skin oversails startling white render walls, recalling earlier Scots harled castles and reinforcing the fenestration, language and boldness of form.

The interiors feature a concentration of exhilarating contrasts: pends; bridges; cavities; pierced incisions. Great halls and intimate rooms make for a rich variety of spaces - each seeming to embrace the collection. Light is funnelled to the depths of the plan, drawing one towards its source overhead and towards a raised rooftop dish. Here, in this large pot that cradles native plant species, your place in this city, within time and in history, is presented, stark against the steadfast magnitude of the Edinburgh rockscape.

This building declares itself with chutzpah and an underlying academic rigour. It recalls the fastidious search for meaning that monasteries once represented, but with a modern vigour. As a visitor, you are counterpointed in a tension between ancient, present and with glimpses towards a far future.

Dundee Contemporary Arts

Nethergate, Dundee

Richard Murphy Architects

SELECTED BY COMPETITION in 1996, Richard Murphy Architects rose to the challenge with gusto, delivering a building that fulfils its primary functions whilst honouring its civic obligations.

By physically placing the public functions at the heart of the complex, visitors are invited into the art world. 'L'-shaped in plan, the building nudges into the public realm and guides visitors towards its entrance with an enticing curve set against a bold oversailing prow-roof, projecting over a large recessed doorway. The street is continued into the plan where a social café space is situated, from which the other primary spaces are reached.

Galleries, cinemas, shop, research spaces and printmaking workshops all have a presence within this public hub. The architects have created a lively internal street that is the beating heart of the complex. The success of this model is demonstrated in these thriving social areas.

Integrating existing buildings into the scheme, the architect, Richard Murphy, has cleverly created a dialogue with the former brick warehouses. New wall planes skim alongside interdependent brick planes. New and old both declare their respective independence while coming together to create a whole far greater than the sum of its parts. Patinated copper sheeting gives the buildings a radiant complexion, in contrast with the brick and brilliant white walls – large canvasses for light.

A credit to its architect and an insightful client, DCA proves that good architecture exists when the users' requirements are carefully considered and exceeded. There can be few, perhaps no, challenges for a more popular public building anywhere in Scotland.

Dundee Contemporary Arts (DCA)
© Keith Hunter

Homes for the Future: The Green

Lanark Street, Glasgow
Elder and Cannon Architects

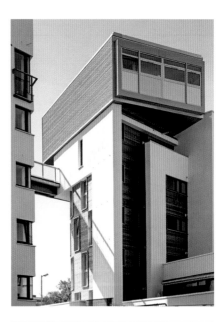

GLASGOW'S DESIGNATION AS THE UK City of Architecture and Design in 1999 drove forward several initiatives with an enduring legacy. One such project is Homes for the Future, near the eastern fringes of the Saltmarket where it gives way to the enormous Glasgow Green on the banks of the River Clyde. A masterplan was drawn up by Page\Park Architects to insert contemporary, mixed use housing into this brownfield area. Several architectural practices designed the various buildings. One of the most distinctive is Elder and Cannon's 'The Green', which gleefully creates a gateway from public green to the more secluded heart of the housing masterplan.

A seven-storey block responds to the street and screens a lower block to the rear. The street façade is capped with penthouse flats including an individual, cranked and cantilevered box acting as a hinge to the corner. This is underscored by an elegant 'skydeck' bridge which connects to the upper storeys of its neighbouring block by Rick Mather Architects.

Façade treatments complement the geometries of the components of the block: timber takes the filleted corner and rear blocks; glass clads the south; planar surfaces are rendered and profiled panelling differentiates the penthouses.

The daily lives of inhabitants have been well considered by the architects. Each flat is planned with a natural flow and healthy proportions between primary spaces. Subsidiary accommodation and circulation have also had critical attention – with rooflights throwing light down sculpted service risers creating more pleasant transitory moments.

This is a somewhat unorthodox housing scheme that offers a bold urban concept. It is an experiment that has largely paid off. More importantly, it creates well-mannered, comfortable homes.

The Green
© Keith Hunter

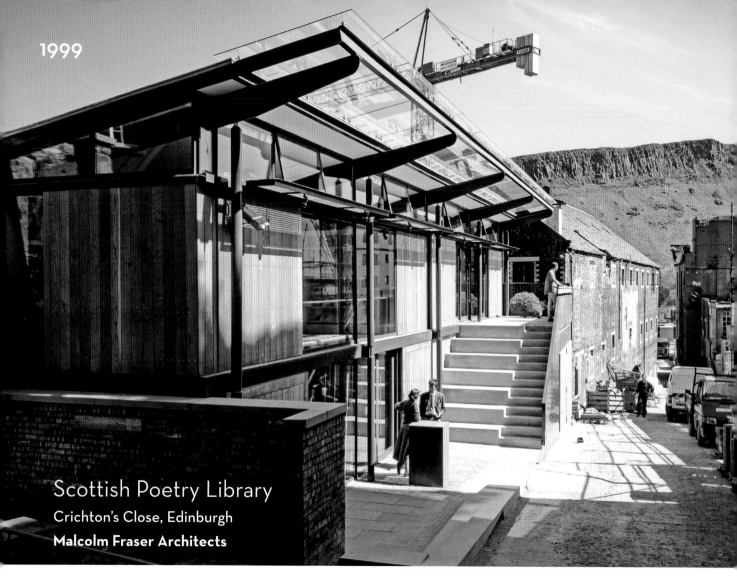

Scottish Poetry Library
Crichton's Close, Edinburgh
Malcolm Fraser Architects

THE HISTORIC OLD TOWN of Edinburgh is an apt location to host a poetry library. Our romantic nation has contributed richly to literary civilisation, much offered by our pantheon of poets. Therefore in the early 1990s when the Scottish Poetry Library sprang into existence, it quickly became apparent that a dedicated home

for its 36,000 volumes would be required.

A constrained and restricted site in Crichton's Close was identified, to which Malcolm Fraser Architects' response was inspired. Using the natural slope of this herringbone vennel, the building comprises well-considered basement, ground and mezzanine floors that

splendidly exploit the section to compose a variety of spaces that delineate their uses.

In its original form (recently amended) a forestair and courtyard reading area with lectern offered a civic 'amphitheatre' which invited the passing public into the heart of this building. This external room

Scottish Poetry Library. The interior has since been altered.
© Keith Hunter

was designed as a poetic crucible within which visitors could orientate themselves to Salisbury Crags and the landscape beyond. The palette of materials is robust yet warm, with glazed brick to the base with glass and oak infill panels to the principal façade.

A *brise soleil* filters light entering the reading area, whereas in the heart of the plan a clerestory window is slanted to match neighbouring walls. Circular rooflights provide ambient light to illuminate book storage areas. Following the roof incline, a central staircase leads

users to the upper floor where one can sit, read and contemplate.

This is a marvellously composed and understated gem, an uplifting place where poetry thrives between the covers of its marvellous collection and through the creativity of those who immerse themselves in its spaces.

The Lighthouse as it opened in 1999.
© Keith Hunter

The Lighthouse

Mitchell Lane, Glasgow
Page\Park Architects

COMPLETED IN 1895 BY Charles Rennie Mackintosh while chief assistant with Honeyman and Keppie, the *Glasgow Herald* Building stood vacant from the 1980s until the Glasgow 1999 festival proposed its adaptation as Scotland's Centre for Architecture, Design and the City. Mackintosh's red sandstone original skirts a narrow lane and sports a prominent corner water-tank tower overlooking West Nile Street. A smaller cream brick chimney to the rear service yard serves as the physical root for Page\Park's intervention.

Principal functions of galleries, workshops, conference rooms and a restaurant all occupy the original shell, whose spaces are delineated by slender cast iron columns and the masonry walls of the former warehousing. To connect these spaces a new 'battery pack' extension was built accommodating toilets and vertical circulation with spill-out and small exhibition spaces.

This extension sports a bold copper-clad concrete, curved wall, peeled back to reveal a generous entrance lobby and define an external balcony above. The density of the plan diminishes as visitors ascend higher above neighbouring rooftops, offering splendid abstracted views of the city. A brilliant moment is provided by way of an heroic spiral staircase inserted in the former water-tank tower, where one can observe Glasgow from an external viewing deck. Here, one can see clearly the extension and its cranked, cantilevered observation deck.

Steel security shutters by Andy Scott which, when retracted, form an abstracted image of Margaret Macdonald (Mackintosh's wife), animates the lane. The striking Lighthouse sign by Javier Mariscal bridges the alleyway, alerting passers-by to the building's presence. The Lighthouse has become one of the institutions of Scotland, and has cleverly given new purpose to a handsome building by way of an alluring, complementary addition.

Tramway

Albert Drive, Glasgow

Zoo Architects

GLASGOW'S TRAMWAY'S PAST was utilitarian. Built as a depot for horse-drawn trams in the 1890s, it was transformed into a car workshop then a transport museum before its current iteration as an arts venue – perhaps its most definitive phase.

Behind its sandstone street façade, the existing shell gives way to humble materials and structuring: cast iron columns and transverse beams support timber roof trusses and walls of clay brick segregate the spaces beneath. Zoo Architects consolidated this fabric whilst inserting new elements to bring life to the building and its purpose. The architects have achieved a fine balance between old and new components, whilst articulating a harmonious dialogue between both.

Greeted by an internal spine and generous entrance accommodating box office, staircases, café and spill out spaces, visitors are given tantalising glimpses to the various attractions on offer. The eye is drawn immediately upwards to the roofscape before entering the gallery and theatre spaces. Behind a reclaimed slate-clad extension one enters the marvellously devised Hidden Gardens by NVA and landscape architects City Design Co-operative.

These new interventions are not shy to express their own idiom within the robust original fabric. We see transformation of roughly finished horse ramps into delightfully shallow staircases, or reclaimed timber lining the circulation routes and other insertions. Tramway sets a benchmark for the quirky adaptive re-use of an existing post-industrial building.

The architects have crafted an arts venue with freedom of function: creating space to display, view, interact or simply meander through. In doing so the reading of the post-industrial heritage of this utilitarian building has been given a renewed sense of self – complete with elemental grit, class and poise.

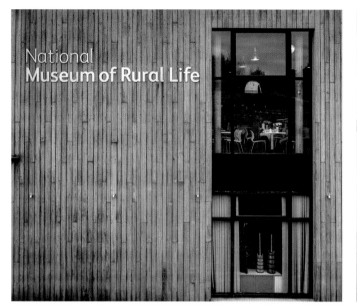

National Museum of Rural Life
© Christopher Marr

National Museum of Rural Life

Wester Kittochside, East Kilbride
Page\Park Architects

IN THE EARLY 1990S THE National Trust for Scotland and National Museums of Scotland came together to create a purpose-built Museum of Rural Life to consolidate a dispersed collection after Wester Kittochside Farm was bequeathed to the Trust. A daring move was proposed by the architects at Page\Park, when they successfully argued to relocate the selected site. This pragmatic consideration allowed for the direct connection of main floor levels to the adjacent ground due to the sloping terrain, providing access for heavy artefacts.

The result is a horizontally articulated building which initially suggests a modest rural barn. A dramatic shift of scale is first suggested with two vertical accents in the form of a handsome chimney and glazed ventilation cowl, aligned to the axis of the entrance bridge that leads to a cavernous hall.

The narration of the collection is via a descending ramp, which coils inwards around halls, galleries and exhibition spaces. This offers glimpses to the outside world through generous splayed openings on its edges. The finale of this journey is revealed at the base of the ramp, with views to the farmscape beyond, framed by the building's exposed structure.

A precast concrete frame harks to the industrial and integrates services and fixings for exhibit display. Each material – whether timber, handmade brick, white textured render or slate – has been expressed frankly, creating a robust and wholesome aesthetic. The quality of this building is staggering when considering its incredibly low budget.

The Museum of Rural Life speaks of Scotland's vernacular transformed into a bold, modern and quietly confident architecture. It displays a valuable aspect of our shared heritage with perfectly balanced quality, flair and intelligence.

Mount Stuart Visitors Centre
© Keith Hunter

Mount Stuart Visitors Centre

Isle of Bute

Munkenbeck + Marshall

THE SEVENTH MARQUESS of Bute deserves praise for opening Mount Stuart, his family home, to the public. The nineteenth century stately house on the Isle of Bute by Sir Robert Rowand Anderson was, each season, attracting around 30,000 visitors who were served by poor accommodation in existing estate buildings. A competition led to the selection of Munkenbeck + Marshall to provide an extension to the Mount Stuart viewing experience.

Tasked with designing a ticket office, gallery, audio-visual facilities, toilets and a restaurant the architects responded with a bold offering. The selected site utilises the slope of a hill, pragmatically serving access requirements but also forming a threshold from car park to the ordered grounds of the house. At ground level a perpendicular approach route intersects the building, where the landscaping gives way to a moat, marking the threshold each visitor must pass.

Boasting a base of crisp, striated timber boards with a blade-like roof floating over a recessed glazed wall, the building speaks of its horizontal articulation. Its simple materials palette allows the building to reflect and blend with its setting, appearing almost ephemeral. This is most evident on the upper external promenade deck, which allows one to take in the landscape or look through to the sky beyond.

The refined structural engineering and rigorous detailing has created slender roof supports, and incredibly thin floor decks so as not to mar the crisp lines of the building. The architects have created a remarkably well-ordered structure which confidently speaks of its time. It is brave architecture, befitting of a family who are custodians of their heritage – yet offered for the public good.

Clavius Building
© Keith Hunter

Clavius Building, St Aloysius College

Hill Street, Glasgow

Elder and Cannon Architects

IN THE 1990S, ST ALOYSIUS College, a private school established in the mid-nineteenth century, required an extension to its Garnethill campus to meet changing demands in education provision. Following a previous junior school development, the College required a new maths, science and technology block. The site identified occupied a corner location, abutting traditional tenements at one end, and meeting the Glasgow School of Art's estate boundary on the other.

Elder and Cannon's bold insertion deals with a challenging programme on a constrained site with considerable skill. To the north a five-storey fully glazed block of 25 classrooms is terminated on its end by a daring system of hung concrete panels. Distinctive diagonal incisions give these façades a degree of delicacy whilst communicating internal life to the adjacent streetscapes.

The masonry walls are enhanced further with glass between planar elements. The full height glazing to classrooms, as well as providing generous proportions is a move that creates inspiring learning spaces. It also opens up the school to its urban environment and beyond. This fastidious attention to detail is exemplary, and contributes to the school's dialogue between its teaching, history and context. To the south the scale drops to relate to lower neighbours, hence, the section is exploited to accommodate varied double-height social spaces, circulation routes and a garden.

In rising to a difficult challenge, both architect and client have achieved an exceptional building. As a good urban citizen it is respectful to its area. The Clavius Building speaks of its era and provides its pupils and teachers with truly outstanding learning and teaching spaces.

The Scottish Parliament

Canongate, Edinburgh

EMBT / RMJM

THE CONSTRUCTION OF SCOTLAND'S new Parliament buildings celebrated the reconvening of that institution after a near three-century hiatus. Selected, ostensibly for their highly individual approach, Enric Miralles and Benedetta Tagliabue, in conjunction with Scottish architects RMJM, suggested a profoundly personal and unique proposal that captivated the collective imagination. As Miralles commented; "After all, parliament is just a different way of sitting together".

Setting out a collage of rocks, stems and leaves, Miralles suggested that the building should represent Scotland as a landscape. The Parliament takes root at the base of Salisbury Crags and flows towards the city like bulging veins beneath a turf skin with a series of tense contour tracks, creating an open, public amphitheatre. This gathering space then predicates the geometry of the debating chamber, establishing it as the heart of the complex.

Integrating into the herringbone plan of Edinburgh through the orthogonal

MSP office block (featuring the distinctive 'think-pod' window seats) the Parliament's sinuous forms are allowed to more freely jostle for position. The incorporation of Queensberry House also connects the campus to the historic Canongate and provides an urban edge to the sublime garden lobby. Through a thrilling symphony of spatial sequences, this hall leads up to the debating chamber in a dramatic crescendo.

The material choices, embedded with significance and meaning, lend the buildings a cohesion and quality. Recognisable as belonging to our Parliament, extraordinary motifs are deployed on façades, fixtures and fittings to permit multiple readings, like many of the country's other epic and legendary artworks.

This is highly charged architecture of allegories, signs and symbols, representative of a progressive and modern ideal of Scotland.

The Scottish Parliament
© Keith Hunter

Helen Kendrick

HELEN KENDRICK, PROGRAMME Manager for the Institute for Future Cities at the University of Strathclyde, came to Scotland in 2004 to work on the conservation of Charles Rennie Mackintosh's tearooms for Glasgow Museums. She has spent over a decade working with architecture and design projects in Scotland for a range of institutions including The Lighthouse and the former Royal Commission on the Ancient and Historic Monuments of Scotland. Helen has curated a number of architecture and design exhibitions in Glasgow, presented papers internationally looking at Glasgow's heritage and is Glasgow's co-representative for the pan-European heritage group the Reseau Art Nouveau Network. She is the author of the publication *Glasgow Interiors* (2014) which charts the city's architecture and design evolution from the 1800s to the early twentieth century.

2006-2015

ESSAYS BY HELEN KENDRICK

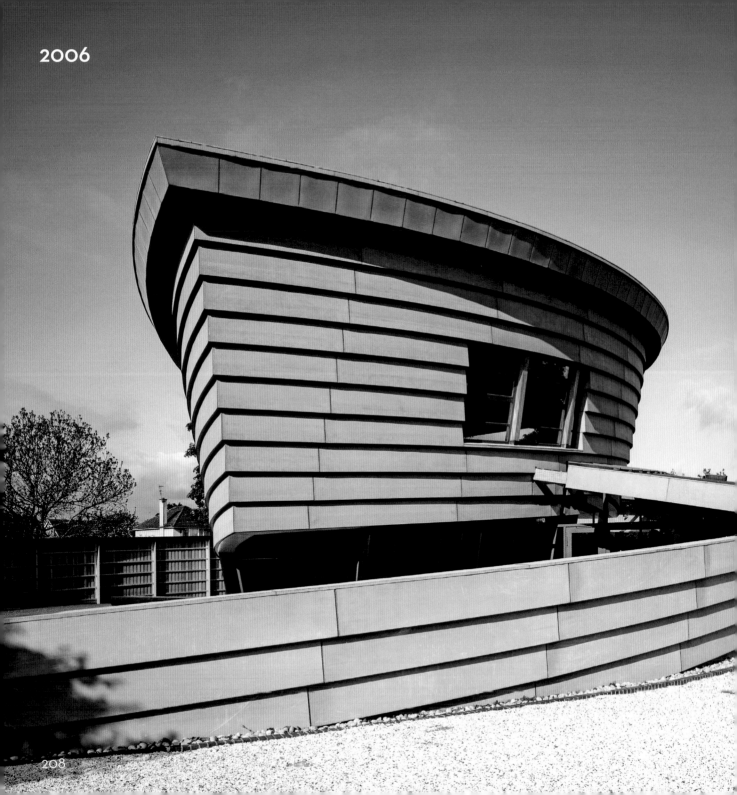

Maggie's Highlands

Raigmore Hospital, Old Perth Road, Inverness
Page\Park Architects

MAGGIE'S CENTRES PROVIDE invaluable support to people with cancer and their families and friends. Founded in Scotland, their contribution to contemporary architecture over the last two decades has been huge.

Maggie's Highlands at Raigmore Hospital in Inverness represents a design collaboration between Glasgow architects Page\Park and acclaimed architectural critic and landscape designer Charles Jencks. Jencks is a co-founder of Maggie's, which follows ideas about cancer care originally developed by his late wife Maggie Keswick Jencks. This centre was developed to deliver an interconnected meeting of landscape and built form and sought to "blur boundaries between internal and external spaces, enclosure and openness". The centre sits between two spiral mounds within the landscape, creating a trilogy of linked forms, with the building's angled walls clad in striking green copper.

The architects described designing space within an enclosing wall which would provide the opportunity for people to step outside yet still remain within the controlled, private and safe environment of the centre. This important 'breathing' space, is set apart from the activity of the internal spaces and rooms. The intimate garden surrounds the centre, connecting into its heart. In fact, in this elegant and contemplative environment, the interior space also flows and connects into the garden, the sharing of shape and pattern blurring the edges.

The first Maggie's Centre opened in Edinburgh in 1996. Since then Maggie's has continued to grow, with seventeen centres in the UK and abroad. The centres are synonymous with innovative, world-leading design. Architects involved in their creation have included Norman Foster, Frank Gehry, Rem Koolhaas and Richard Rogers. Maggie's Highlands' many accolades include the RIAS Andrew Doolan Best Building in Scotland Award for 2006.

Maggie's Highlands
© Keith Hunter

Pier Arts Centre
Victoria Street, Stromness, Orkney
Reiach and Hall Architects

LIGHT SPILLS INTO THIS beautiful, crisply delineated building by day and glows from it at night. The heritage of the old Stromness waterfront is simultaneously respected and enhanced by Reiach and Hall's dramatic and widely acclaimed re-working of the Pier Arts Centre. When it re-opened in 2007, the press and visitors were entranced by a building which simultaneously houses the collection within and becomes a crucial part of it.

The original buildings for the gallery, which was founded in the 1970s, comprised an eighteenth century house fronting Stromness Main Street with a nineteenth century storehouse built onto the pier behind it. Reiach and Hall's re-development included refurbishing the existing historic buildings and adding a striking new 'shed', which has more than doubled the display space of the gallery and enabled the addition of a shop and offices.

The bold contemporary architecture befits the Pier's contents. The gallery has one of the most important collections of twentieth century British art in the UK, gifted to the people of Orkney by radical British art collector and peace activist Margaret Gardiner. A close friend and supporter of the St Ives School in Cornwall, she had built up her collection during the 1930s and 40s.

In more recent years, the gallery has developed the collection with contemporary works by celebrated Scottish artists including Turner Prize nominees Christine Borland and Callum Innes, cementing its place as one of Scotland's most innovative artistic institutions. The gallery has been credited with breathing new life into the Orcadian arts scene and inspiring a new generation of artists. Reiach and Hall's re-development has won numerous awards, most notably the RIAS Andrew Doolan Best Building in Scotland Award in 2007.

Pier Arts Centre

ABOVE

© Crown Copyright Historic Environment Scotland. Licensor canmore.org.uk

OPPOSITE PAGE

© Gavin Fraser

John Hope Gateway

Royal Botanic Garden of Edinburgh, Arboretum Road, Edinburgh
Cullinan Studio

JOHN HOPE GATEWAY, the Royal Botanic Garden of Edinburgh's (RBGE) 2009 biodiversity and information centre, occupies the site of the former Botanics shop and includes exhibitions showcasing the scientific work of RBGE, classrooms, a restaurant and retail space. The eponymous John Hope, former Keeper of the Botanics, was a leading eighteenth century botanist and teacher.

London-based architectural practice Cullinan Studio was awarded the project. The building offers a showcase for the firm's interest and specialism in innovative architectural solutions for environmental protection and energy conservation.

Energy efficiency measures and renewable technologies in the building include a wind turbine, biomass-fuelled boiler, solar collectors for hot water, and photovoltaic panels. Natural, local materials feature extensively throughout, particularly timber (Scottish wherever possible) which is used in both structure and finishes. The building takes an organic form, fitting unobtrusively into the Botanic Gardens. It has no obvious 'front' or 'back' since it is intended that it be approached from different directions and levels. The extensive use of timber gives the visitor a powerful feeling of 'connection' with nature, enhanced by the glass walls that reduce the visual barriers.

The architects commented that stone, timber, concrete and glass are incorporated within the building in ways that exploit their own inherent qualities. The stacked Caithness stone connects the building into the landscape of the Botanic Gardens. The timber glulam roof, the most dramatic element within a series of superbly composed built forms, is set on pencil-thin steel columns – the most slender that the engineering of the building would allow. The subdivision of the space below into a series of timber bays creates separate zones for the wide range of activities which take place here and the glass wall opens the building onto the new biodiversity garden.

Shettleston Housing Association Offices

Pettigrew Street, Glasgow
Elder and Cannon Architects

FOR OVER THIRTY YEARS, Elder and Cannon Architects has successfully breathed new life into historic buildings in and around Glasgow through creative and contemporary architectural interventions. Buildings such as the celebrated Castlemilk Stables (restored in 2007) showcase this ability, seen here also in the, multi award-winning, Shettleston Housing Association Offices in the east end of the city.

The re-working of the early twentieth century red sandstone Co-operative Halls in Shettleston, allied with a new extension providing additional reception, meeting and office spaces (plus an envy-inducing roof terrace for the staff), unites two very different built forms. The concrete-finned extension is a dramatically contemporary response to the older building that successfully integrates within the historic context. It follows the traditional five-bay rhythm of the Edwardian block and aligns its roof level with the neighbouring eaves. The scale of the modern elevation, extending beyond its volume to match its historic neighbour, adds to the sense of 'prestige' of this important development.

Inside the building, interventions include the addition of timber pods and glass-walled meeting rooms, giving staff and clients a high quality, modern environment within the original offices. This is an architecturally and culturally significant site for Glasgow and an inspired reworking of a good example of the city's proud Edwardian commercial buildings (home, since the 1970s, to Shettleston Housing Association, which now manages 2300 homes in the area).

The building won the 2011 RIAS Andrew Doolan Best Building in Scotland Award, with judges commenting: "This is an important building for Shettleston. There is no question that new architecture of this quality will contribute to enhanced pride of place and further high quality development in the area".

Shettleston Housing Association Offices
© Andrew Lee

The Houl
© Andrew Lee

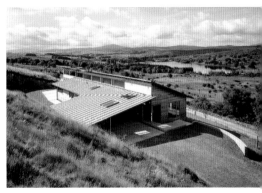

The Houl

St John's Town of Dalry, Castle Douglas
Simon Winstanley Architects

THE HOUL, AN ELEGANT single-storey family home in the Water of Ken valley in Dumfries and Galloway, is a contemporary re-interpretation of the traditional Scottish longhouse. Designed by (and for) local architect Simon Winstanley, it is also 'net zero carbon', utilising a range of traditional and modern sustainable construction techniques to achieve its zero carbon credentials.

Sustainability measures include an air-source heat pump, wind turbine, heat recovery ventilation, and high levels of insulation, including triple glazing. However, this commitment to sustainable construction does not compromise the architectural styling. As *Wallpaper** magazine commented on the building's completion in 2011: "This is no hotchpotch sum of eco parts – far from it. Indeed the 'green' hardware (apart from the wind turbine) has been deliberately concealed, allowing the integrity of the simple yet subtle 'God is in the detail' design to be in no way compromised by its performance enhancing technologies".

The main building's steel-framed structure is broken up with walls clad in cedar weatherboarding (now silvery-grey) and topped with a seamed zinc roof, cantilevered on all sides to create additional shelter. The large proportion of (triple-skinned) glass allows extensive views over the spectacular local landscape to the hills of Rhinns of Kells. Clerestory windows to the rear of the house allow the morning sunlight to pour through the rest of the home.

At the heart of the building, a functional yet beautiful red room divider, incorporating a log-burning stove, provides a splash of colour in an otherwise largely monochrome and wood interior. Full-height sliding doors allow the principal space to spill out to the timber deck, a transition into the landscape beyond.

 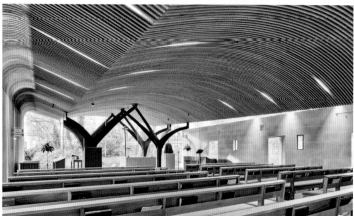

The Chapel of St Albert the Great
© Chris Humphreys

The Chapel of St Albert the Great

George Square, Edinburgh
Simpson & Brown Architects

MAKING A BOLD AND BEAUTIFUL statement in the rear garden of a townhouse within one of Edinburgh's most historic squares sits the Chapel, completed in late 2012 for St Albert's Catholic Chaplaincy and Friary for the Dominican Order (The Order of Preachers). This new building replaces the Chaplaincy's former worship space on the upper floor of one of the George Square townhouses, providing ground floor and disabled access via a new entrance off George Square Lane.

The striking architecture of the new chapel, with its glass walls and 'green' roof, connects it directly with the natural environment of its garden setting. The link between architecture and nature continues in the interior, with timber slats and four, tree-like, Corten steel supporting columns, two internal, two external, which connect, drawing the natural setting into the building.

The architects Simpson and Brown have commented that both the choice

of materials and the building's form were crucial in determining their design approach. The sedum roof connects the building to its garden setting, and minimises its visual impact from above. The entirely glass west wall connects the chapel with the changing seasons, which play an important part in the worship calendar.

The use of glass in the building extends to clerestory glazing, ventilator windows and rooflights, giving both natural light and air circulation. The use of mirrors cleverly filters daylight through oak slats along the length of the chapel. These oak walls also add an important, if unplanned, element to the atmosphere of the building. As the architects themselves pointed out, the smell of oak as you enter the chapel was not part of their original plan but now add another sensory experience to the delight of this very special building.

House No. 7
© David Barbour

House No 7

Scarinish, Tiree

Denizen Works

WHEN LONDON-BASED architect Murray Kerr's parents purchased an historic blackhouse on Tiree, their plans were for restoration and a traditional extension. They intended to live there for roughly half the year. However, their plans had to be re-thought drastically when surveys revealed that the original structure was unstable and beyond repair.

Kerr's revised concept was to rebuild the house in traditional style, adding two extensions modelled on agricultural sheds referencing the local vernacular. The result is a living-house, guesthouse, and inter-linking utility wing (particularly useful for cleaning the exposed island's omnipresent sand from shoes). The materials used contrast soft with hard, curved with angular and include stone, corrugated fibre cement and steel. The stylish interiors feature much use of timber.

The mostly flat (and frequently windy) island presented unique complications,

including that the new house, in common with its historic predecessor, was likely be buried up to the window cills in wind-blown sand at certain times of year. Shelter had to be created on all sides, while still allowing a level of interaction with the natural environment and, particularly, exploiting the abundant sunlight of the southern coast of the Inner Hebrides. Tiree enjoys the most hours of sunlight of anywhere in the UK.

The house is now well known and celebrated, both on Tiree and internationally, having featured in *The New York Times*, *Elle Decor Italia* and *Casa Vogue*. The building has won numerous prizes including 2014's *Grand Designs* Home of the Year and the 2014 RIBA Stephen Lawrence Prize whose judges considered it "an intelligent and witty response to the functional and logistical challenges of location, orientation and isolation".

The Turf House
© Nigel Rigden

The Turf House

Kendram, Kilmaluag, Isle of Skye
Rural Design

THIS PRIVATE HOME ON the romantic Hebridean Isle of Skye, recently voted fourth best island in the world by *National Geographic*, is something of a reality TV star, having featured in the popular UK television series *Grand Designs*. The building is designed to blend seamlessly into the landscape at the northernmost tip of Skye with minimal visual impact, reflecting the client's brief and also a key requirement for gaining planning approval. Its turf roof acts almost as camouflage and the larch cladding on the exterior is already starting to bleach and turn silver with time, again helping the building to blend into its environment.

Inside, the home is essentially a single volume with an open plan kitchen/living room and a gallery bedroom platform above. The bathroom, services and main bedroom are ingeniously tucked in below this mezzanine. Windows maximise the dramatic views, with the view of the headland being framed through a glazed wall, hooded to provide additional shelter. The only source of heat is a wood-burning stove. A ventilation system with heat recovery, as well as high levels of insulation and airtightness maximises energy efficiency.

Built on a modest budget, this two-bedroom family home was praised by *Grand Designs* presenter, the designer Kevin McCloud, as "such an original building in such a traditional place." After twelve series of the programme, he declared the Turf House one of his "favourite houses ever". The building, sitting snugly beneath its turf roof, has attracted well-deserved international interest and industry recognition.

Maggie's Lanarkshire
© David Grandorge

Maggie's Lanarkshire

Monklands District General Hospital, Monkscourt Avenue, Airdrie
Reiach and Hall Architects

THAT THERE ARE TWO Maggie's Centres featured in this book is testament to the central role high quality design plays in the Maggie's care programme and ethos. Architects for Maggie's projects give their time for little or nothing. There is invariably a high level of personal investment. These centres include some of the most experimental, innovative and influential healthcare buildings of the past two decades.

Reiach and Hall, a practice founded in Edinburgh in the 1960s, had a solid pedigree for this Maggie's commission in Lanarkshire after completing the award-winning Beatson Cancer Research Centre in Glasgow in 2008 and their supremely elegant 2009-11 designs for Stobhill Hospital.

Observing that "a Maggie's brief is challenging for many reasons", the architects have explained that the Maggie's centres provide a different kind of care from conventional medical facilities. Set in domestic scaled buildings and neither house nor hospital, the plans of the Maggie's centres tend to revolve around the kitchen table, the traditional and familiar focus of most homes, Of this centre they said: "Our plan too develops from the kitchen table outwards to the courtyards, the trees and beyond".

Book-ended by mature lime trees (the remains of the woodland belonging to the demolished Tudor-style Airdrie House) and enclosed by a perforated wall of pale Danish brick, the composition was conceived within a walled garden. The development is punctuated with a series of courtyards, outdoor seating areas, and a spring that animates the entrance with the sound of running water. In the inner courtyards (open to the sky) are gold-stained 'sun-catchers' designed by the brilliant international lighting designer, Jonathan Speirs.

Laurieston Transformational Area Housing
© Andrew Lee

Laurieston Transformational Area Housing

Cumberland Street, Glasgow

Elder and Cannon Architects; Page\Park Architects

GLASGOW'S LATE NINETEENTH AND early twentieth century industrial expansion resulted in streets of poorly built, overcrowded homes in the Gorbals, later demonised in the book *No Mean City*. The 1960s comprehensive redevelopment solutions to the poor quality housing in the area, including the Queen Elizabeth Square 'multis' by Basil Spence (demolished 1993), subsequently also failed. The Crown Street Masterplan in the early 1990s and the later plan for Laurieston, inspired by Crown Street's success, heralded a new dawn for Gorbals.

Public sector housing has changed dramatically over recent decades.

The most recent addition to the area, on cleared land between Gorbals and Tradeston, is this large scale, deservedly award-winning, public housing development that learns lessons from the past fifty years. High quality contemporary design and materials provide a range of affordable homes for rent.

Delivered as the first phase of the masterplan for Laurieston, the project, which is a collaboration between Glasgow practices Elder and Cannon and Page\Park, is a collection of 200 properties, including townhouses and flats, all following in Glasgow's long tradition of tenemental homes. Back gardens face onto communal garden space, and the front gardens of townhouses include off-street parking. West-facing gardens are larger to maximise the light provided by the evening sun. The project was praised by the RIAS as an exemplar of successful place making and "a triumphant piece of urban regeneration."

It is testament to local and national capacity for architectural innovation, imagination and confidence that the Gorbals area has so comprehensively re-invented itself as a desirable place to live. Much of the credit for that transformation must go to exemplary design projects such as this.

Acknowledgements

THE ORIGINAL INSPIRATION FOR the first *Scotstyle* exhibition and publication in 1984 came from the architect Kit Campbell RIAS. The idea was taken up, with characteristic gusto, by then Royal Incorporation of Architects in Scotland (RIAS) Secretary, Charles McKean Hon FRIAS. A team of experts was gathered, chaired by the Incorporation's President, John Richards CBE and public nominations were sought for the nation's top 150 buildings (to mark the 150th birthday of the RIAS' sister institute, The Royal Institute of British Architects).

The exhibition toured throughout Scotland and the original publication, written by the very young Fiona Sinclair is still a much-valued research resource – and a very good read.

This new, 2016, version of *Scotstyle* marks the centenary of the RIAS, as part of the Festival of Architecture 2016. Again the public was asked to nominate. This time the expert panel also became the authors of the exhibition and the book.

This publication and the touring exhibition which it was written to accompany were co-edited by Neil Baxter Hon FRIAS and Fiona Sinclair FRIAS. Design was by the RIAS' hugely talented graphic designer, Jon Jardine. Jon also gathered most of the images and copyright permissions. In addition to the brilliant photographers who have very generously contributed their images without charge (all credited within the book) we are very grateful to Glasgow School of Art, the Scran and Canmore online photo libraries (which operate under Historic Environment Scotland's banner). The Instagram community in Scotland has helped fill many image gaps and Grant Bulloch FRIAS has been particularly generous with his time and photographic talents. Again, credits for the Instagram photographers' images feature in the book.

The sponsors of the Festival of Architecture, particularly our headline sponsors, EventScotland (part of VisitScotland), Creative Scotland (whose additional support enabled our Scotland-wide Scotstyle tour), ScotRail and the Herald & Times Group merit special thanks. Their generous support has helped to bring our year-long Scotland-wide Festival into being.

Iain Dickson PPRIAS would like to thank the Friends of Craigtoun Park.

Ruairidh Moir RIAS would like to thank David Reat RIAS and Gordon McGregor for their insights on the Scottish Parliament, David MacRitchie FRIAS for his advice on the Museum of Rural Life and John Doherty FRIAS and Gary Mair at Elder and Cannon for their guidance on the Clauvius Building and Homes for the Future: The Green.

The co-editors would very much like to thank Charles McKean Hon FRIAS for continuing to inspire so many good things, their co-authors for the quality of their writing (and being so tolerant of the editorial interference), David Dunbar PPRIAS, Chair and Karen Cunningham, Director: Festival of Architecture 2016 for their guidance and advice, Willie Watt PRIAS for his continuing support, Jon Jardine for being such an inspiring and talented designer and Carol-Ann Hildersley for her endless patience and nurturing of this book through its long gestation.

Credits

EDITORS Neil Baxter Hon FRIAS and Fiona Sinclair FRIAS

BUILDING SELECTION AND TEXT
Neil Baxter Hon FRIAS
Helen Kendrick
Ranald MacInnes
Sarah Pearce
Frank Walker OBE FRIAS

Iain Dickson PPRIAS
Euan Leitch
Ruairidh Moir RIAS
Fiona Sinclair FRIAS
Andrew P K Wright OBE PPRIAS

DESIGN AND PHOTOGRAPHIC RESEARCH Jon Jardine

PHOTOGRAPHY
David Barbour
Barnabas Calder
Jamie Howden
Keith Hunter
Matt Laver
Christopher Marr
Jimmy Reid
Nigel Rigden
Fiona Sinclair FRIAS
Andrew PK Wright OBE PPRIAS

Grant Bulloch FRIAS
David Grandorge
Chris Humphreys
Jon Jardine
Andrew Lee
Ruairidh Moir RIAS
Jean O'Reilly
James Roy
Michael Wolchover

ARCHIVE PHOTOGRAPHY
The Glasgow School of Art
Morris and Steedman
Scran

Canmore
Nicoll Russell Studios

Bibliography

Alexander, Christopher / Chermayeff, Serge, *Community and Privacy: Toward a New Architecture of Humanism*, 1963

Arts Council, The and the RIBA, *Architecture Today* exhibition catalogue, 1961

Bailey, Rebecca, *Scottish Architects' Papers: A Source Book*, 1996

Bain, Susan, *Holyrood: the Inside Story*, 2005

Banham, Reyner, *The New Brutalism*, 1966

Benson + Forsyth with contributions from Sir Colin St John Wilson RA, Prof. Duncan MacMillan and John Allan, *Museum of Scotland*, 1999

Campbell, Louise / Glendinning, Miles / Thomas, Jane, *Basil Spence: Buildings and Projects*, 2012

Canmore - www.canmore.org.uk

Cantacuzino, Sherban, *Great Modern Architecture*, 1966

Cruft, Kitty / Dunbar, John / Fawcett, Richard, *The Buildings of Scotland: Borders*, 2006

Curtis, William JR, *Modern Architecture Since 1900* (first published 1982, third edition 1996)

Edwards, Brian, *Basil Spence, 1907-1976*, 1995

Frampton, Kenneth, *Modern Architecture: a Critical History* (first published 1980, fourth edition 2007)

Gifford, John / McWilliam, Colin / Walker, David / Wilson, Christopher, *The Buildings of Scotland: Edinburgh*, 1984

Gifford, John, *The Buildings of Scotland: Fife*, 1988

Gifford, John, *The Buildings of Scotland: Highland and Islands*, 1992

Gifford, John, *The Buildings of Scotland: Stirling and Central Scotland*, 2002

Glendinning, Miles (ed), *Rebuilding Scotland: The Postwar Vision, 1945-1975*, 1997

Glendinning, Miles / MacInnes, Ranald / MacKechnie, Aonghus, *The History of Scotland's Architecture*, 1996

Glendinning, Miles, *Modern Architect: the Life and Times of Robert Matthew*, 2008

Gomme, Andor and Walker, David, *Architecture of Glasgow*, 1968

Haynes, Nick, *Building Knowledge: An Architectural History of the University of Glasgow*, 2013

Higgs, Malcolm / Riches, Anne / Williamson, Elizabeth, *The Buildings of Scotland: Glasgow*, 1990

Historic Scotland, *Scotland: Building for the Future*, 2009

Kinchin, Juliet and Kinchin, Perilla (with Neil Baxter), *Glasgow's Great Exhibitions*, 1988

Long, Philip and Thomas, Jane (eds), *Basil Spence: Architect*, 2007

MacMillan, Duncan, *Scotland's Shrine: The Scottish National War Memorial*, 2014

McKean, Charles, *The Scottish Thirties: An Architectural Introduction*, 1987

McKenzie, Ray, *Public Sculpture of Glasgow*, 2002

McWilliam, Colin, *The Buildings of Scotland: Lothian*, 1978

Our Bank: The Story of the Commercial Bank of Scotland, 1941

Paxton, Roland and Shipway, Jim, *Civil Engineering Heritage: Scottish Lowlands and Borders*, 2007

Pehnt, Wolfgang (ed), *Encyclopaedia of Modern Architecture*, 1963

Petit, Jean, *Un Couvent de Le Corbusier*, 1961

RCAHMS, *Creating a Future for the Past: the Scottish Architects' Papers Preservation Project*, 2004

RIAS Illustrated Architectural Guides: Borders and Berwick (Charles Strang, 1994); *Central Glasgow* (Charles McKean, David Walker and Frank Walker, 1993); *Dumfries and Galloway* (John R Hume, 2000); *Dundee* (Charles McKean and David Walker, 1993); *Edinburgh* (Charles McKean, 1992); *The Kingdom of Fife* (Glen L Pride, 2000); *The North Clyde Estuary* (Frank Arneil Walker / Fiona Sinclair, 1992); *Stirling and the Trossachs* (Charles McKean, 1985).

Rogerson, Robert WKC, *Jack Coia: His Life and Work*, 1986

Savage, Peter, *Lorimer and the Edinburgh Craft Designers*, 1980

Sinclair, Fiona, *Scotstyle: 150 Years of Scottish Architecture*, 1984

Skriver, Poul Erik (ed), *Guide to Modern Danish Architecture*, 1965

Sloan, Audrey with Murray, Gordon, *James Miller: 1860-1947*, 1993

Smith, GE Kidder, *The New Architecture of Europe*, 1961

Tagliabue, Benedetta, *EMBT Enric Miralles Benedetta Tagliabue: Works in Progress*, 2006

The Dictionary of Scottish Architects - www.scottisharchitects.org.uk

Walker, Frank Arneil, *The Buildings of Scotland: Argyll and Bute*, 2000

Weaver, Sir Lawrence, *The Scottish National War Memorial* (undated)

Webb, Michael, *Architecture in Britain Today*, 1969

Index